AIRPORT
SPOTTING GUIDES

EUROPE

Guidelines for spotting locations and facilities at some of Europe's busiest and most popular airports.

Matthew Falcus

First Edition 2008

ISBN 978-0-9559281-0-9

The information in this book is true and complete to the best of our knowledge. All recommendations are made without any guarantee on the part of the Publisher, who also disclaims any liability incurred in connection with the use of specific details or content within this book.

© DestinWorld Publishing Ltd 2008

British Library Cataloguing-in-Publication Data
A catalogue record for this book is available from the British Library.

Published by DestinWorld Publishing Ltd.
www.destinworld.com

All photographs in this book are © Matthew Falcus

Contents

Europe's Main Airports

Europe's Main Airports cont…

Europe's Low Cost Airports

Introduction

This guide has been put together following many years spent visiting and researching some of Europe's most popular airports for watching aircraft. Whilst airports today are constantly evolving and changing their buildings, environment and security rules, it is the intention that this book gives a good overview of all the available facilities at each airport. Naturally situations change regularly, with new airlines and routes started, and old ones dropped. Terminal facilities are also being updated and modernised at a steady pace, and facilities provided for enthusiasts are dwindling every year.

Many locals have been consulted in the preparation of this book in addition to personal research to ensure the information presented is as up-to-date as possible. Updates from readers are always welcome through our publisher site. These will be incorporated into the next update.

The guides in this book attempt to cram as much important information as possible within the pages, so that every aspect of an enthusiasts visit is covered, from hotels with aircraft views to relevant local attractions and airfields.

Most aircraft enthusiasts today make use of the many low-cost airlines flying to many destinations at affordable prices. Never has it been more affordable to take quick trips to the continent. For this reason, this book includes shorter guides to a number of the more popular low-cost hubs on the Continent.

It should always be remembered when visiting airports that enthusiasts adhere to security rules and restrictions. Fences should never be climbed over, and escape routes should never be blocked. In most cases, airport security is happy to allow logging and photography if you inform them in advance. For this reason you will find the general customer service telephone numbers for each airport listed. Beware, however, that rules differ from country to country. In France, photography of aircraft is not permitted at Paris Charles de Gaulle airport without a pass, and in Italy police officers are known to move on spotters regularly.

The maps in this book are entirely produced to aid the text, and should not be used for any real-life navigation purposes.

Amsterdam (Schiphol)
Netherlands

AMS | EHAM

Tel: +31 207 940 800

Web: www.schiphol.nl

Passengers: 47.8 million (2007)

Overview

Schiphol today is one of the world's largest and busiest airports, having cemented its place in the aviation world at an early age despite the relatively small size of the Netherlands. The low-lying country was once covered by much more water than currently, and the Schiphol site is testament to that. Haarlem Lake was once a vast expanse of water used by merchant ships and ferries servicing the town of Haarlem from the middle ages up until 1848 when the decision was made to drain the lake, thus creating more countryside. The resultant land, which was flat and around 10m below sea level was soon realised to be the perfect location for a landing field following the invention of powered flight. The first aircraft landed here in August 1916.

Many phases of expansion have brought about the airport we see today, with the most recent additions including the opening of the sixth runway, and a smaller addition to the terminal for the use of the ever-present low-cost airlines.

Most European airlines serve Amsterdam today, as well as the major internationals and many cargo airlines. The airport is an important venue for enthusiasts, and has always provided facilities that allow logging and photography both at the terminal and around its perimeter.

On the site formerly occupied by the Fokker company, a great deal of maintenance and business jet activity can also be witnessed, although this is a little harder to accurately log.

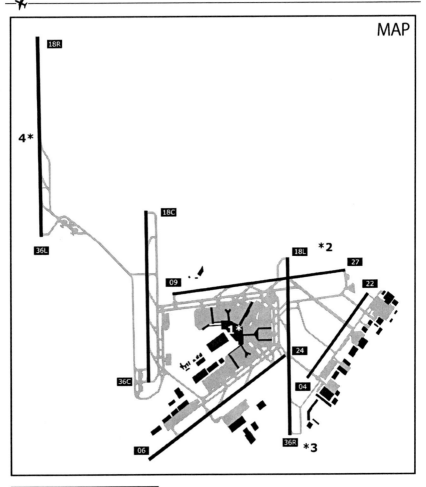

MAP

Frequencies

118.100	Tower
118.275	Tower
119.225	Tower
119.900	Tower (Start)
118.075	Approach/Departures
119.050	Approach/Departures
121.200	Approach/Departures
126.675	Approach/Departures
118.800	Radar
120.550	Radar
129.300	Radar
121.700	Ground
121.800	Ground/Apron
121.975	Clearance Delivery
108.400	ATIS

Runways

04/22	6,608x148 ft / 2,014x45 m
06/24	11,483x148 ft / 3,500x45 m
09/27	11,329x148 ft / 3,453x45 m
18C/36C	10,826x148ft / 3,300x45m
18R/36L	12,467x198ft / 3,800x60 m
18L/36R	11,155x148 ft / 3,400x45 m

Spotting Locations

1. Panorama Terrace

This official terrace is located along the top of the central terminal area. Although it has been reduced in size recently because of airport expansion, it still commands good views across piers B to D and most of the runways. Aircraft that are not seen arriving can usually be seen taxiing at some point. Entrance to the terrace is free. It can be reached through the entrance hall to Schiphol Central, and is well-signposted. Facilities include an indoor cafe, restaurant and bar, and arrivals screens which usually give aircraft registrations. Opening times: from last Sunday in October 9am-5pm; from last Sunday in March 7am-8pm.

2. McDonalds

One of the official viewing areas is located alongside a McDonalds restaurant to the north of Runway 27. Most of the airport's movements can be seen here, as well as the maintenance and business jet ramps. Photography is not perfect here due to the south-facing aspect, however some aircraft are at close quarters on the runway.

3. Runway 36R

When landings are on this runway, this spot offers great photographs. In the industrial estate next to the threshold of the runway, turn right at the gas station, where there is plenty of parking space. On the afternoon, drive past the approach lights and take the second right for a spot with the sun behind you.

4. Runway 18R/36L

Two official viewing locations have been sited alongside the new sixth runway. Naturally a car or cycle is required to get there. There are spots to park, and good views of traffic arriving or departing on the runway.

Airside Spotting

When flying through Schiphol, the single-terminal operation makes viewing fairly easy. You can wander between piers once through security, and large windows provide views of most parked aircraft and some of the runways. Pier D offers the best views of the business jet and cargo ramps. The commuter ramp is obscured from all piers except B, however.

Nearby Attractions

National Aviation Theme Park Aviodrome

Pelikaanweg 50, 8218 PG Lelystadt Airport ☒ +31 900 2846376 ☒ www.aviodrome.nl

Located at Lelystadt Airport, 45 minutes from Schiphol. This museum has many restored historic aircraft, with particular emphasis on Dutch aviation. Most notable are the last flying DC-2 in the world, the first Fokker F27 Friendship built, flying Antonov AN-2 and Catalina, and a former KLM Boeing 747-206B (SUD). Pleasure flights are often available in the flying aircraft.

Rotterdam Airport

Rotterdam Airport is a 45 minute drive to the south. A viewing area within the terminal will give views of most of the movements, which include KLM and VLM commuter aircraft, low-cost flights by Transavia, and many business and private movements.

Airlines

Adria Airways	China Airlines	Israir	SAS
Aer Lingus	China Southern Airlines	Jade Cargo Airlines	SATA Internacional
Aeroflot	Clickair	Japan Airlines	Singapore Airlines
Afriqiyah Airways	Continental Airlines	Jat Airways	Singapore Airlines Cargo
Air Astana	Corendon Airlines	Jet2	Sky Airlines
arberlin	Croatia Airlines	Kenya Airways	SkyEurope
Air Cairo	CSA Czech Airlines	KLM	Sterling
Air France	Cyprus Airways	Korean Air	Sun D'Or
Airlinair	Delta Air Lines	LOT Polish Airlines	Sun Express
Air Malta	easyJet	Lufthansa	Surinam Airways
Air Nostrum	easyJet Switzerland	Malaysia Airlines	SwissInternationalAirLines
Air Transat	Egyptair	Malév Hungarian Airlines	Syrian Arab Airlines
Alitalia	El Al	Martinair	TACV Cabo Verde Airlines
AMC Airlines	Emirates Cargo	MAT Macedonian	TAP Portugal
ArkeFly	EVA Air	Meridiana	Transavia
Arkia	Finnair	MyAir	Tunisair
Armavia	Fly Air	Northwest Airlines	Turkish Airlines
Atlas Air	Flybe.	Nouvelair	UkraineInternationalAirlines
Atlas Blue	FlyLAL	Olympic Airlines	United Airlines
Austrian	Focus Air Cargo	Onur Air	US Airways
Blue1	Georgia Airways	Pegasus Airlines	VLM Airlines
Bmi	Great Wall Airlines	PIAPakistanInternational	Vueling
bmibaby	Iberia	Polar Air Cargo	West Air Sweden
British Airways	Icelandair	Rossiya	
Bulgaria Air	Inter Airlines	Royal Air Maroc	
Cathay Pacific	Iran Air	Royal Jordanian	

Hotels

Etap Hotel

Schipholweg 185, 1171 PK BADHOEVEDORP ☒ +31 20 348 3533 ☒ www.etaphotel.com
One of the cheapest of the hotels at Schiphol. The Etap is also conveniently located next to the McDonalds viewing location. Alternatively, the central terminal area is a five minute drive. There is a free airport shuttle for guests.

Ibis Amsterdam Airport

Schipholweg 181, 1171 PK BADHOEVEDORP ☒ +31 20 502 5100 ☒ www.ibishotel.com
Next door to the Etap is the Ibis hotel, which offers similar convenience for spotting locations, and a free shuttle to the terminal.

Hilton Schiphol Airport Hotel

Schiphol Boulevard 701, 1118 BN SCHIPHOL ☒ +31 207 104 096 ☒ www.hilton.com
A slightly more expensive option is the Hilton, which has the benefit of a central location amongst the central terminal area. It overlooks the airport, but has very few views of any of the action.

Athens (Eleftherios Venizelos International)

Greece

ATH | LGAT

Tel: +30 (0) 21 03 53 00 00
Web: www.aia.gr
Passengers: 15.1 million (2006)

Overview

Athens' Eleftherios Venizelos International Airport is a brand new facility to the east of the city which was built to replace the original Hellenikon airport in the city centre, which was limited by space and unhappy neighbours.

The new airport opened in 2001, and was built with plenty of space for expansion. It features two long parallel runways and a single terminal building. It is the busiest airport in Greece, and home of Olympic Airways.

At either side of the terminal building are ramps for commuter aircraft, cargo, business and private aircraft, and maintenance.

Athens acts as a hub for flights in south eastern Europe. Many carriers from surrounding countries serve the airport. Most major airlines in Europe serve the airport, including some low-cost carriers, and some from North America and the Far East send aircraft daily. The visitor is sure of an interesting mix on any visit.

MAP

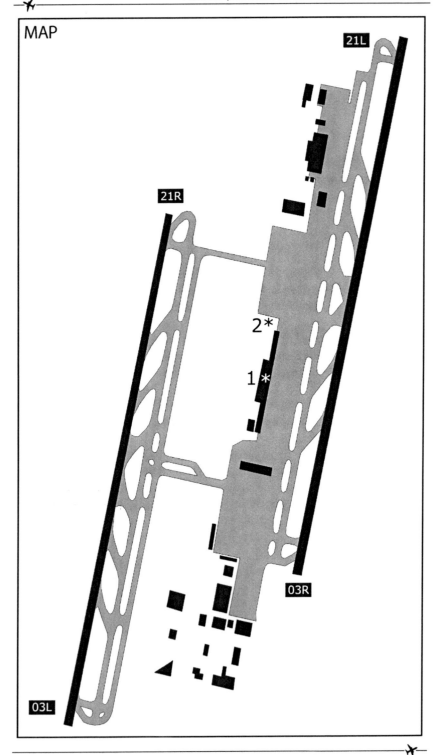

Frequencies

118.625	TowerRW03R/21L
122.100	Tower
136.275	TowerRW03L/21R
119.100	Approach
129.550	Approach
121.750	Ground North
121.800	Ground West
121.900	Ground East
121.950	Ground South
118.675	Clearance
136.125	ATIS

Runways

03R/21L 13,123x148ft / 4,000x45m
03L/21R 12,467x148ft / 3,800x45m

Spotting Locations

1. McDonalds Restaurant

On the 4th floor of the terminal, this location has plenty of seating and large windows give views over the gates, taxiways and eastern runway. Photography is easy with a 200mm lens. The aspect can be a problem in winter, but is not a problem in the summer. Most movements will be seen from here.

2. Departures Level

Walking outside the terminal at Departures level, turn right and you'll find an area with views over the other runway. There are shaded seats here to enjoy the view, although photography is fairly difficult. Walking a little further to the end of the pedestrian area gives some views over the executive jet ramp.

3. Perimeter Roads

Various roads lead around parts of the airport perimeter from the central road area around the terminal. These can offer various vantage points of aircraft on the runways and on short final to land depending on directions in use. Security patrols are common, however.

Airside Spotting

Once airside, the terminal has windows at most gates which allow aircraft to be logged.

Security

The airport prefers that spotters inform security personnel in advance of their planned activities. They are known to be accommodating within the terminal building, however security is tight around the perimeter.

Airlines

Aegean Airlines	clickair	Malév Hungarian Airlines
Aeroflot	Continental Airlines	MEA Middle East Airlines
AeroSvit Airlines	CSA Czech Airlines	MyAir
airberlin	Cyprus Airways	Norwegian Air Shuttle
Air China	Delta Air Lines	Olympic Airlines
Air France	Donbassaero	Qatar Airways
Air Malta	easyJet	Royal Jordanian
Air Moldova	Egyptair	SAS
Air One	El Al	Saudi Arabian Airlines
Air Transat	Emirates	Singapore Airlines
Albanian Airlines	Georgian Airways	SkyEurope
Alitalia	Germanwings	Sterling
Alpi Eagles	Gulf Air	Swiss International Air Lines
Armavia	Iberia	Syrianair
Austrian Airlines	Ilyich-Avia	Tarom
Blue1	Jat Airways	Thai Airways
British Airways	KD-Avia	Tunisair
Brussels Airlines	KLM	Turkish Airlines
Bulgaria Air	KrasAir	Uzbekistan Airways
Carpatair	LOT Polish Airlines	Vueling
Centralwings	Lufthansa	

Hotels

Sofitel Athens Airport

19019 Spata ☒ +30 21 03 54 40 00 ☒ www.sofitel.com
Situated at the airport complex, very close to the terminal. A smart and modern hotel, like the airport itself, with fantastic service. Higher rooms have views of the movements which can be read off with binoculars. Fairly expensive, though booking in advance will mean cheaper rates.

Nearby Attractions

Hellenikon Airport

The former Athens airport has been largely redeveloped since its closure in 2001. There are, however, a group of stored airliners here formerly operated by Olympic Airlines, including a Boeing 727-200, 737-200, 747-200, and a BAC 1-11.

Barcelona
Spain

BCN | LEBL
Tel: +34 902 40 47 04
Web: www.aena.es
Passengers: 32.8 million (2007)

Overview

Barcelona is Spain's second city, and since the Olympic Games of 1992 has had an airport to match this status. It is located 10km from the city centre in the area of El Prat, and opened on the site in 1918. Today it is home to the world's busiest air route, between Madrid and Barcelona.

Despite living in the shadow of Madrid Barajas, Barcelona has held its own with an extensive network of domestic, intra-European, and long-haul flights by a number of carriers. The main Spanish carriers all have a strong presence here, as do Europe's low-cost airlines. In addition to this, Baracelona is served by a number of long-haul airlines – particularly to North and South America. Singapore Airlines is the main operator to Asia.

A new terminal is currently being built between the two parallel runways which will greatly relieve pressure on the existing structures and allow further expansion. It is unknown whether this will feature any official spotting facilities. The new building will open in 2008, and will see capacity rise to 70 million passengers per year.

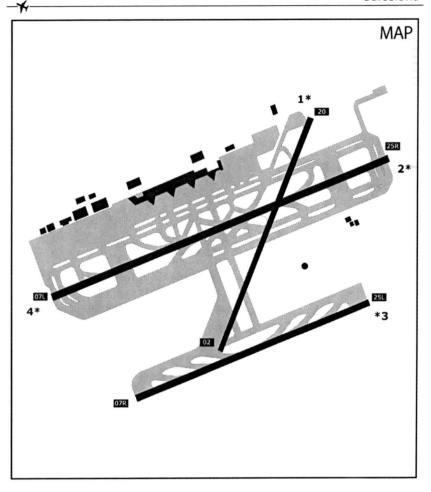

MAP

Frequencies

118.100	Tower
118.050	Approach
119.100	Approach
124.700	Approach
125.250	Approach
126.500	Approach
127.700	Approach
121.700	Ground
121.800	ClearanceDelivery
118.650	ATIS

Runways

02/20	8,333x148ft / 2,540x45m
07R/25L	8,727x197ft / 2,660x60m
07L/25R	11,654x148ft/3,552x45m

Spotting Locations

1. Runway 20

From the terminal, follow the main road out and take the first exit. Turn right on to Ronda del Sud and follow until you reach a roundabout. Go straight over, then go right at the next roundabout. At the next roundabout, find somewhere to park. This spot is not ideal for photography, but aircraft can be logged landing and lining up on Runway 20.

2. Runway 25R

From the first location, continue along Carretera de l'Aviació. Turn right at the first roundabout, and go straight over the next one. You will soon come to the approach lights for Runway 25L. Here, there are benches and some shade. Aircraft are at close quarters as they approach this runway. Plenty of people congregate here, and cyclists pass regularly. A ladder is needed for good shots over the fence.

3. Runway 25L

Follow the road from the Runway 25R location until you reach the end of Runway 25L. Again, there are places to park. Aircraft approaching the runway are very close to you and fine for photographs. A ladder is needed for good shots over the fence.

4. Runway 07L

When the 07 direction is in use, this spot offers the best chances of photography. From the terminal, follow the main road and take the first exit, heading south on the C-31 in the direction of Castelldefels. Take the first exit from this motorway, and soon you will see aircraft approaching the runway. Take the exit on to Carretera de l'Accés al Camping, and park on the rough ground immediately.

Airside Spotting

The windows in the main terminal offer some good opportunities for spotting once airside. Photography is possible in most cases, and all movements can be seen.

Hotels

Best Western Hotel Alfa Aeropuerto

Calle K Entrada Mercabarna, Zona Franca, 08040 Barcelona
+34 93 33 62 564 ✉ www.bestwesternalphaaeropuerto.com

Fairly affordable and comfortable, and less than two miles from the terminal. It offers shuttles to the airport, but no views of aircraft movements from its rooms.

Tryp Barcelona Aeropuerto

Parque de Negocios Mas Blau II, Prat de Llobregat, Barcelona 08820
+34 93 37 81 000 ✉ www.somelia.com

Slightly closer to the airport, and offering free shuttles around the clock. The hotel is smart and modern, and fairly affordable. No views of aircraft movements.

Airlines

Adria Airways	Continental Airlines	Onur Air
Aer Lingus	CSA Czech Airlines	Pegasus Airlines
Aeroflot	Delta Air Lines	Portugalia
Aerolineas Argentinas	DHL Air	Rossiya
Aeroméxico	easyJet	Royal Air Maroc
Air Algérie	easyJet Switzerland	Royal Jordanian
Air Comet	Egyptair	S7 Airlines
Air Europa	El Al	SAS
Air France	Emirates Cargo	SkyEurope
Air Malta	Estonian Air	Smart Wings
Air Nostrum	Eurofly	Sol Airlines
Air One	FedEx Express	Spanair
Air Slovakia	Finnair	Sterling
Air Transat	FlyGlobespan	Sun D'Or
airBaltic	Futura	Swiftair
airberlin	Germanwings	Swiss International Air Lines
Alitalia	Iberia	Syrian Arab A
Alpi Eagles	Iberworld	TAP Portugal
American Airlines	Iceland Express	TAROM
Arkia	Icelandair	Thomas Cook Airline
Atlas Blue	Jade Cargo	TNT Airways
Austrian Airlines	Jet2	Transaero
Avianca	KD-Avia	Transavia
Blue Air	KLM	Tunisair
Blue Line	Lagun Air	Turkish Airlines
Blue1	LOT Polish Airlines	Ukraine International Airlines
bmibaby	Lufthansa	UPS
British Airways	Luxair	Ural Airlines
Brussels Airlines	Meridiana	US Airways
Bulgaria Air	Monarch Airlines	VIM Airlines
Cargoitalia	MyAir	Vueling
Cargolux	Neos	Windjet
clickair	Norwegian Air Shuttle	Wizz Air
Condor	Nouvelair	XL Airways

Nearby Attractions

Gerona-Costa Brava Airport

The region's low-cost airport, dubbed Barcelona Girona despite being over 90km from the city. Naturally the main operator is Ryanair, however a number of business jets and light aircraft can be seen on any given visit. It is also popular with charters. Roads to either side of the terminal offer views over the runway thresholds.

Brussels (National / Zaventem)
Belgium

BRU | EBBR

Tel: +32 27 53 77 53
Web: www.brusselsairport.be
Passengers: 17.8 million (2007)

Overview

Brussels is the largest and busiest airport in Belgium, serving the capital and headquarters of the European Union. It continues to increase passenger throughput year-on-year, despite the demise of national carrier SABENA, and competition from the Eurostar train link.

The reorganisation of the national carrier has seen a number of changes at the airport, and interesting airlines to see operating the principal routes throughout Europe, and to North America and Africa. Most of the important carriers, both local and long-haul, serve Brussels. Low-cost carriers are not as prevalent.

Cargo was always important to Brussels, with FedEx and DHL traditionally having bases here. This has changed somewhat since the early 1990s, and there are now much fewer cargo operations here. You may still catch unusual freighters from far-off parts, however.

The airport doesn't provide any official spotting locations, however there are a number of locations where movements can be logged – especially for those with a car. Airside, the airport is very good for spotting.

Spotting Locations

1. Car Park
Walk outside the terminal and head to the left, where the multi-storey car park can be found. The top level gives views over the southern apron and hangar areas. Photography is possible from here.

2. Water Tower
The road running around the perimeter has a spot close to the end of Runway 25L

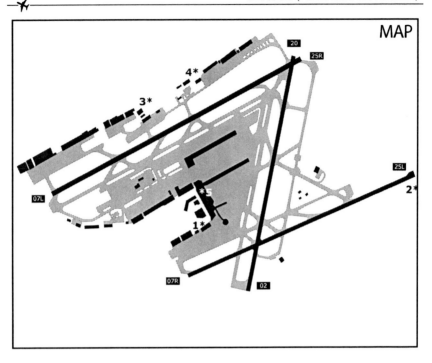

MAP

Frequencies

118.600	Tower
120.775	Tower
118.250	Approach
120.100	Approach
122.500	Approach
127.575	Final 25L
129.725	Final 25R
121.950	Clearance
126.625	Departure
118.050	Ground
121.875	Ground
112.050	ATIS
114.600	ATIS
117.550	ATIS
132.475	ATIS

Runways

02/20	9,800x164ft / 2,987x50m
07R/25L	10,535x148ft / 3,211x45m
07L/25R	11,936x148ft / 3,638x45m

which offers good shots of landings and aircraft on the runway. It is so named because of the nearby water tower. To reach the location, take the A201 motorway away from the terminal, and the R0 motorway south. Leave this after a few miles for the E20 East. Take the first exit left on to Mechelsesteenweg (N227). Before the tunnel under the runway, turn right on to Tervuursesteenweg. You will see parked cars and spotters at the end of the runway.

3. General Aviation Area

Leaving the terminal area, follow signs for General Aviation. Turn right at the roundabout, and then turn left after 100m. Just past the General Aviation terminal is a parking area. From here, views of the cargo aircraft are possible, though photography is not perfect. Aircraft departing Runway 25R can easily be seen after lifting off.

4. Cargo Area

Following directions for the General Aviation Area, taking another left and following the road. Turn right in the direction of Haacht on the N21. Turn right at the second traffic lights, following Cargo signs. Go right at the roundabout and left at the Post building. Turn right after 100m and park next to the security gate. A short walk reveals the parked cargo aircraft at close quarters. Some pictures of aircraft taxiing are possible.

5. Wingtips Restaurant

The spotting location recommended by the airport itself is the Wingtips Restaurant, located on the fourth floor of the terminal, which is not airside. There are fairly panoramic views over the central apron area here, and many aircraft will taxi past. Photography is possible. Some aircraft will not be seen from here, particular on the cargo ramps.

Airside Spotting

There are many large windows around gates in all areas, and a number of cafes and lounge areas watch over the movements. The newer satellite pier obstructs views from the older part of the terminal, but most movements will pass it eventually anyway.

Hotels

Sheraton Brussels Airport

Brussels National Airport, Brussels 1930 ☒ +32 27 10 80 00 ☒ www.sheraton.com

This is the best hotel option for spotting aircraft at Brussels Airport. Although expensive, rooms have views over the aprons. It is a short walk from the terminal and mult-storey car park location. Photography is not possible from the rooms, however.

Novotel Brussels Airport

Da Vinci Laan 25, Bedrijvenzone Diegem-Vuurberg, Diegem 1831
+32 27 25 30 50 ☒ www.novotel.com

Affordable hotel, located less than 2km from the terminals, with free shuttles. It is also located a short distance from the Runway 18 spot.

Airlines

Adria Airways	Cyprus Airways	Northwest Airlines
Aegean Airlines	Delta Air Lines	Olympic Airlines
Aer Lingus	DHL Air	Qatar Airways
Aeroflot	Eastern Airways	Royal Air Maroc
Afriqiyah Airways	Egpytair	SAS
Air Algerie	El Al	Saudi Arabian Cargo
Air Canada	Estonian Air	Singapore Airlines
Air France	Ethiopian Airlines	Singapore Airlines Cargo
Air Malta	Etihad Airways	SkyEurope
Air Senegal	EVA Cargo	South African Airways
Air Transat	easyJet	SriLankan Airlines
airBaltic	easyJet Switzerland	Sterling
Alitalia	Finnair	Swiss International Air Lines
All Nippon Airways	Flybe.	Syrianair
American Airlines	Gulf Air	Turkish Airlines
Atlas Blue	Hainan Airlines	TAP Portugal
Austrian Airlines	Iberia	TAROM
Blue Air	Jat Airways	Thai Airways International
British Airways	Jet Airways	Thomas Cook Airlines Belgium
Bmi	JetairFly	Tunisair
Brussels Airlines	KLM	US Airways
Bulgaria Air	LOT Polish Airlines	Ukraine International Airlines
CSA Czech Airlines	Lithuanian Airlines	United Airlines
clickair	Lufthansa	VLM Airlines
Continental Airlines	Malév Hungarian Airlines	Vueling
Corendon Airlines	Malmö Aviation	
Croatia Airlines	MyAir	

Nearby Attractions

Musée Royal de l'Armée
Jubelpark 3, Brussels 1000 ⊠ 32 (0) 27 37 78 33 ⊠ www.klm-mra.be

A museum in the Parc de Cinquantenaire in downtown Brussels which has a number of aircraft on display. These include a Boeing 707 and Sud Aviacion Caravelle formerly of Sabena, a DC-3 and a Junkers Ju-52. Open Tuesday to Sunday 9am to 12pm and 1pm to 4.45pm. Admission free.

Charleroi Airport
The local low-cost airport, and a base for Ryanair. Charleroi is 28 miles from Brussels. Buses run regularly from the city centre. There are some spotting locations around Charleroi.

Liege Airport
Liege is the cargo hub of Belgium (one of the biggest in Europe), and a base of TNT Airways. It is particularly busy through the night. Expect occasional Russian cargo aircraft. There are a few spotting locations. Liege is easily reached by road, and is some 60 miles to the east of Brussels.

Cologne/Bonn (Köln/Bonn)
Germany

CGN | EDDK
Tel: +49 (0) 22 03 40 40 01
Web: www.airport-cgn.de
Passengers: 9.9 million (2006)

Overview

The major draw of Cologne/Bonn for many enthusiasts is the busy UPS hub which has been based here since 1986. In addition to this, the airport is one of Germany's busiest, serving the former capital city of Bonn, and a large catchment area which stretches into Luxembourg, Belgium and the Netherlands.

Cologne/Bonn was quick to embrace the low-cost revolution. Today many of the flights are operated by these airlines, including foreign examples such as easyJet, Wizz Air, and home-grown airlines Germanwings and TUIfly, which have bases here.

The airport has two terminals. Terminal 1 handles Lufthansa, Star Alliance and Germanwings movements, whilst all others use Terminal 2. Elsewhere, the large cargo terminal, maintenance area, and German Air Force ramp can be found between the two parallel runways. One of these runways is a designated landing site for the NASA Shuttle.

Another note to enthusiasts is the storage area at Cologne/Bonn which has held a number of decaying aircraft for many years, as well as a few temporary resident. For anyone looking to pad out their Fokker F-27 logs, look no further than the area past the cargo terminal.

MAP

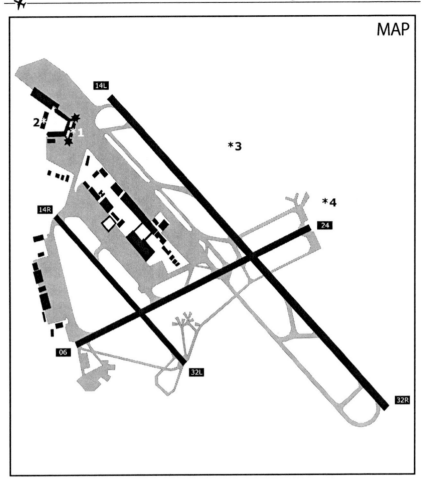

Frequencies

124.975	Tower
121.050	Approach
126.325	SurveillanceRadar
121.850	Clearance
121.950	Ramp
121.725	Ground
112.150	ATIS
119.025	ATIS

Runways

06/24	8,067x148ft / 2,459x45m
14R/32L	6,112x148ft / 1,863x45m
14L/32R	12,516x197ft/3,815x60m

Spotting Locations

1. Terminal Observation Platform

The official terrace is provided within Terminal 1 between areas B and C. These cover views over the apron and runway operations, and can usually be relied upon for logging aircraft at the cargo terminal. Photography is generally good when the windows are clean. The terrace is open daily from 6.30am to 10pm (except in poor weather) and is free.

2. Terminal 2 Car Park

The top level of the Terminal 2 Car Park is another spot with views over the passenger terminal aprons. It can also help with identifying some of the cargo aircraft, and also gives views to the stored aircraft at the far end of the airfield.

3. Perimeter Road

For those with a car, take the road motorway leading away from the terminal, but immediately take the first exit and turn right, and right at the lights on to Alte Kölner Strasse. Follow this road for a few miles as it loosely follows the perimeter through the forest. Look for areas to park on the right. Various footpaths lead to the fence from here, giving views across Runway 14L/32R to the passenger and cargo terminals.

4. Runway 24

Following Alte Kölner Strasse a little further brings you to the end of Runway 24. There are limited places to park. This spot will give excellent photographs of aircraft on short finals for this runway.

Airside Spotting

Both terminals have great views once airside of aircraft at the terminal you're in. Terminal 1 is best as you can see the aircraft from both terminals using the taxiways and runways. The same cannot be said for Terminal 2.

Resident Airframes

OE-LSE CRJ200LR, ex Styrian Spirit
OE-LSF CRJ200LR, ex Styrian Spirit
D-AELC F-27-600 ex WDL Aviation
D-AELD F-27-600 ex WDL Aviation
D-AELE F-27-600 ex WDL Aviation
D-AELF F-27-600 ex WDL Aviation
D-AELH F-27-400 ex WDL Aviation
D-AELI F-27-600 ex WDL Aviation
D-ADOP F-27-600 ex WDL Aviation
D-BAKC F-27-600 ex WDL Aviation
D-BCEA, marked D-CGN 01 FH-227J ex Brit Air
D-EKQA, marked D-CGNF Piaggio 149D fire service
31+29 Fiat G.91R-3 airbase entrance
23+98 F-104G inside airbase
70+43 UH-1D inside airbase

Airlines

airberlin	easyJet	MEA Middle East Airlines
Air Europa	Flightline	Nouvelair
Air Malta	Freebird	Onur Air
Arkia	Germania	Pegasus Airlines
Atlas International	Germanwings	SAS
Austrian Airlines	Hamburg International	Sky Airlines
Blue Air	Hellas Jet	South African Airways
Bluewings	Inter Airlines	Spanair
Bmi	InterSky	Sun Express
Bulgarian Air Charter	Iran Air	TuiFly.com
Cimber Air	Israir	Tunisair
Cirrus Airlines	Karthago Airlines	Turkish Airlines
Condor	KTHY	UPS
Continental Airlines	KLM	Wizz Air
CSA Czech Airlines	Lufthansa	

Hotels

Holiday Inn Cologne-Bonn Airport

Waldstrasse 255, Cologne 51147 ✆ +49 (0) 22 03 56 10 ⌨ www.holidayinn.com

Conveniently located for the airport and motorway. Rooms can be expensive at certain times. The hotel is not ideally suited for viewing, although some upper rooms may offer views of the passenger apron and aircraft on finals to Runway 14R.

Copenhagen (Kastrup)
Denmark

CPH | EKCH
Tel: +45 (0) 32 31 32 31
Web: www.cph.dk
Passengers: 21.4 million (2007)

Overview

Copenhagen is one of Europe's oldest airports. It became popular as a hub early in its career with the formation of Scandinavian Airline System (SAS), and the introduction of trans-polar flights from America. Today it is one of the busiest airports in Scandinavia.

Perched at the southern end of the city on a peninsula, space was always a problem at Copenhagen. However, three runways are available meaning movements are rarely restricted.

The airport also has three terminals. Terminal 1 handles all domestic flights. Terminal 2 handles most of the general traffic at the airport, and most international airlines. Terminal 3 is used by SAS and its Star Alliance partners for international flights – by far the busiest users of the airport. A number of cargo airlines use the airport's facilities also.

Copenhagen has a few locations for watching aircrafts; however it is regarded as a fairly frustrating airport for those without a boarding pass.

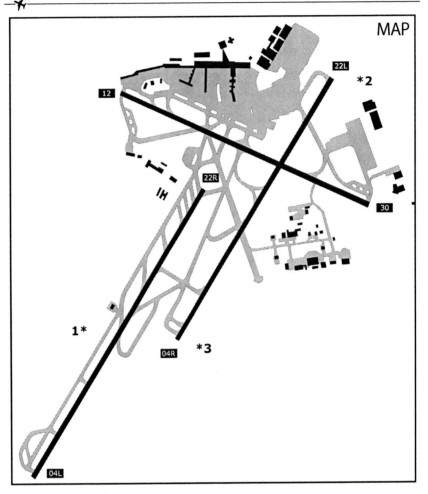

MAP

Frequencies

118.100 Tower
118.575 TowerDepartures
118.700 Tower
119.350 Tower
119.900 Tower
118.450 Approach
119.800 Approach
121.600 Apron
121.725 Ground
121.900 Ground
120.250 Departure
124.975 Departure
122.850 Departure ATIS

Runways

04R/22L 10,827x148ft/3,300x45m
04L/22R 11,811x148ft/3,600x45m
12/30   10,072x148ft/3,070x45m

Spotting Locations

1. Flyvergrillen

By far the most popular spotting location at Copenhagen is located alongside Runway 22R/04L. The Flyvergrillen is a café and burger bar, and has a dirt mound alongside which offers views over the movements on the runways and taxiways. It is acceptable for photography on afternoons. To reach the spot, walk out of Terminal 1 and turn left at the catering buildings. You can also drive this route. It takes 30 minutes to walk.

2. Runway 22L

From Terminal 3, walk to the right. At the roundabout with McDonalds and the filling station, turn right and walk past the DHL buildings. Follow the path round past the end of the runway until you reach a suitable spot. This location is good for photographs of aircraft on short finals on mornings and early afternoons. You will also be able to log aircraft at all terminals and the cargo area.

3. Runway 04R

A good spot can be reached by car when aircraft are using Runway 04R. Follow the road away from the terminals and past the Flyvergrillen spot. Eventually, join Englandsvej southbound and go through the tunnel under the airport. After emerging at the other side, take the first left on to Nordre Kinkelgade. Follow this to the left through the small village, and eventually you will come to the spot alongside the fence. A stepladder is required for good shots. Aircraft at the terminals are too far away to accurately read off.

Airside Spotting

Once airside it is possible to get some good views of the action. This goes for all three terminals. The best location is at the end of Pier B. Piers A, C and D also have opportunities, especially around gates A11/12. Photography is possible through the windows.

Resident Airframes

OY-STD Caravelle, ex Sterling
OY-BVH Fokker F-27, ex Business Flight
OY-BZW Metro II, ex Muk Air
LN-PIP Douglas DC-8 ex Chico Dan

Websites

www.cphaviation.dk

Nearby Attractions

Malmö Sturup Airport

Despite being over the border in Sweden, Malmö is very close to Copenhagen and just a short drive across the impressive Oresund Bridge. The airport is used extensively by low-cost carriers such as Sterling and Wizz Air. It is also served by Malmö Aviation and SAS. There are limited views from the terminal and car parks of parked aircraft. A Caravelle can be found on the fire dump.

Airlines

Adria Airways	Croatia Airlines	Middle East Airlines
Aer Lingus	Czech Airlines	Norwegian Air Shuttle
Aeroflot	Danish Air Transport	Novair
airberlin	Delta Air Lines	PIA Pakistan International
Air Baltic	easyJet	Rossiya
Air France (Brit Air)	Estonian Air	Singapore Airlines
Air Greenland	Finnair	Skyways Express
Air One Alitalia	Flynordic	Sky Europe
Arkia	Iberia	Spanair
Atlantic Airways	Icelandair	Sun D'Or
Austrian Airlines	Iceland Express	Swiss International Air Lines
Blue1	Iran Air	Syrian Arab Airlines
bmi	Jat Airways	TAP Portugal
British Airways	Jet Air	Thai Airways International
Brussels Airlines	Jettime	transavia.com
Bulgarian	KLM	Turkish Airlines
Air Charter	LOT Polish Airlines	SAS
Cimber Air	Lufthansa	Sterling
Continental Airlines	Malév Hungarian Airlines	Widerøe

Hotels

Hilton Airport Hotel

Ellehammersvej 20, Copenhagen 2770 ☒ +45 32 50 15 01 ☒ www.hilton.com

The Hilton is linked to the terminal via a covered walkway. Most even-numbered rooms from the 10th floor up offer views of the aprons, with photography possible. Can be expensive.

Zleep Airport Hotel

Englandsvej 333, Copenhagen 2770

Although it offers no views of aircraft from its rooms, this hotel is very affordable and only a short walk from both the terminal and the café viewing area.

Dublin (Collinstown)
Republic of Ireland

DUB | EIDW

Tel: +353 (0) 18 14 11 11

Web: www.dublinairport.com

Passengers: 23.2 million (2007)

Overview

When built in 1940, the terminal at Dublin's airport was considered to be the best in Europe and won architectural accolades for its designer.

Following the Second World War, the number of services increased rapidly. Three hard runways were laid, and new hangars and other buildings built. A terminal extension could only cope a few years into the long-haul jet revolution, and in 1972 another new building was opened with a capacity of 1.6 million passengers per year. The current main runway 10/28 was opened in 1989.

With the general rise in passenger numbers due to popular routes to London and New York came also the low-cost boom. Local carrier Ryanair dramatically boosted passenger figures with its cheap flights to the UK and Europe, and today has a massive base here. The passenger terminal has required steady expansion, and in 2006 opened its new pier to alleviate pressure.

Sadly no official spotting facilities remain at Dublin, but a number of locations around the perimeter are popular.

MAP

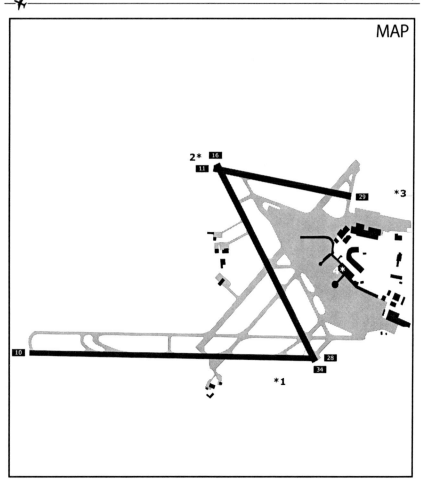

Frequencies

118.600 Tower
119.550 Approach TAR
121.100 Approach
118.500 Surveillance Radar
124.650 South
128.00 Radar
129.175 North
121.800 Ground
121.875 Clearance Delivery
124.525 ATIS
127.575 ATIS

Runways

10/28	8,652x148ft	/ 2,637x45m
11/29	4,393x200ft	/ 1,339x61m
16/34	6,789x200ft	/ 2,072x61m

Spotting Locations

1. Southern Perimeter

Following the road away from the terminal, turn on to Old Airport Road, which follows the perimeter. You'll soon be alongside the main runway, and depending on the direction in use you can find a raised spot which will put you alongside the touchdown zone. Many spotters congregate here. Photography is good, and all traffic will pass you eventually. Follow the road around for spots on the northern side of the runway. Buses heading for Dublin will drop you ½ a mile from this location (Dardistown Cemetery). A car is recommended.

2. Runway 16

Following the perimeter road around will lead you past the fire station and to the threshold of Runway 16. Parking along the side of the road, you can take good photographs here. This runway is not used as much.

3. Maintenance Area

Following the road along the northern perimeter eventually leads back to the terminal area. Just before this, there are some smaller roads and car parks from where the maintenance area can be seen. There are usually a couple of airliners parked here.

4. Inside Terminal

Upstairs in the terminal is the Sky View Café food court. Seating in the McDonalds restaurant and bar area offers a vantage point over part of the aprons and taxiways. The corridor leading to the toilets from here gives views over arriving traffic.

Airside Spotting

All areas of the terminal have some views of aircraft parked at the gates. Be sure to log what you can from piers B and C, which offer good views of the runways and taxiways, before proceeding to the Ryanair pier D, or pier A as you can not go back. The café in the Ryanair pier is a good place to see nearly all movements.

Resident Airframes

EI-CJD 737-204 ex Ryanair fire service

Airlines

Adria Airways
Aer Arann
Aer Lingus
Air Canada
Air Contractors
Air Southwest
Air Transat
airBaltic
American Airlines
Blue Islands
bmi
British Airways
Centralwings
CityJet
clickair
Continental Airlines
CSA Czech Airlines
Delta Air Lines
DHL Air
Estonian Air

Etihad Airways
Eurocypria Airlines
Flybe.
FlyGlobespan
FlyLAL
Germanwings
Iberia
Lufthansa
Luxair
Malév Hungarian Airlines
Monarch Airlines
Ryanair
SATA Internacional
SAS
SkyEurope
Swiss International Air Lines
S7 Airlines
TNT Airways
Turkish Airlines
US Airways

Hotels

Clarion Hotel Dublin Airport

Dublin Airport ☒ +353 (0) 18 08 05 00 ☒ www.clariondublinairport.de

This is the only hotel at Dublin Airport with views of aircraft. This is limited to aircraft landing on Runway 28, and only available from certain rooms. The hotel is a short walk from spotting locations on the perimeter road.

Radisson SAS Great Southern Hotel

Dublin Airport ☒ +353 (0) 18 44 60 00 ☒ www.radissonsas.com

This is a tall hotel set amongst the car parks near the terminal and maintenance area. Some upper rooms may yield views of the aprons and runways. The hotel is fairly expensive.

Düsseldorf
Germany

DUS | EDDL

Tel: +49 (0) 21 14 210

Web: www.dus-int.de

Passengers: 17.8 million (2007)

Overview

Always a popular airport because of the excellent viewing facilities and interesting mix of aircraft, Düsseldorf is also easy to get to with the current spate of low-cost airlines offering services from across Europe.

The current airport developed after the end of the Second World War, when the original was completely destroyed. Most of the current infrastructure was built between the 1950s and 1970s, however in recent years modernisation and expansion has been taking place.

The airport has a single terminal with three piers. An executive terminal is located to the west, whilst a cargo terminal and apron are to the east.

Airlines serving the airport cover a wide variety, with many of Germany's charter and leisure airlines putting in a good number of movements. A number of eastern European carriers also serve Düsseldorf, and long haul routes are offered by Delta, Emirates, Lufthansa, and Northwest Airlines

Interestingly Düsseldorf is capable of handling the Airbus A380, and is Lufthansa's first choice of diversion airport should Frankfurt be unusable. It will not feature in the airport's timetable, however.

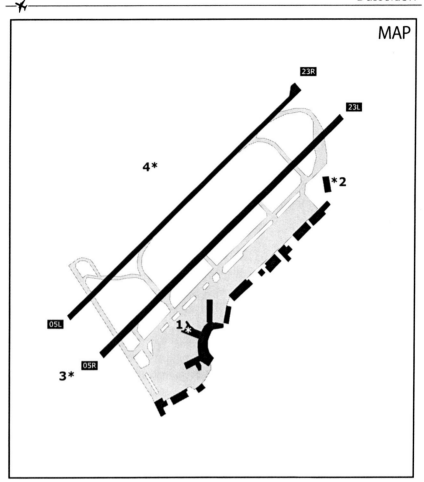

MAP

Frequencies

118.300 Tower
119.700 Tower
119.400 Surveillance Radar
119.700 Surveillance Radar
128.550 Surveillance Radar
124.675 Radar
125.225 Radar
120/050 Approach/DeparturesNorth
128.550 Approach/DeparturesSouth
128.650 Approach
121.900 Ground
121.775 Clearance
115.150 ATIS
123.775 ATIS

Runways

05R/23L 9,842x148ft / 3,000x45m
05L/23R 8,858x148ft / 2,700x45m

Spotting Locations

1. Terminal Observation Deck

This terrace is located above the B pier. It allows visitors to get close to the action, with aircraft parking all around you, and the runways in the near distance. Access is via the third floor of the terminal.

2. Railway Station

The other official observation deck at Düsseldorf is at the railway station to the east of the terminal. It can be reached by the SkyTrain. Here, views of aircraft using the runways can be enjoyed at close quarters, although this is only really of use when 23L/R are being used. The cargo ramp is also nearby.

Both observation areas are open daily from 6am to 9pm (8pm between 28 October and 29 March). A single ticket gives access to both areas, which costs €2 for adults, €1.50 concessions, and €1 for children. Remittance is only valid for three hours, but re-entry is welcome.

3. Runway 5R

A popular spot with locals is under the final approach path to Runway 5R. Follow Flughafenstrasse from the airport, or near the Stockum exit from the A44 Autobahn. Park the car and cross the railway tracks at the station. The path leads north under the approach path, with spectacular views.

4. Runway 5L/26R

A road runs the length of this runway, with various places to stop and get close-up shots of the action. Be careful not to obstruct emergency gates.

Airside Spotting

All three piers inside the terminal offer views through windows of aircraft parked, and give some limited views of the executive and cargo ramps, and the runways.

Airlines

Aegean Airlines	Free Bird Airlines
Aer Lingus	Iberia
Aeroflot	Jat Airways
Aeroflot-Don	Jet2
Afriqiyah Airways	KD-Avia
African Safari Airways	KLM
airBaltic	LOT Polish Airlines
airberlin	LTU
Air France	Lufthansa
Air Malta	MAT Macedonian Airlines
Air Via	Northwest Airlines
Alitalia	Norwegian Air Shuttle
Armavia	Nouvelair
Atlas Air	Olympic Airlines
Austrian Airlines	Onur Air
Bestair	Pegasus Airlines
Blue Wings	Polar Air Cargo
British Airways	Rossiya
Bulgarian Air Charter	Royal Air Maroc
Carpatair	S7 Airlines
Condor	SAS
Croatia Airlines	Sky Airlines
CSA Czech Airlines	Sun Express
Delta Air Lines	Swiss International Air Lines
Egyptair	TuiFly.com
Emirates	Tunisair
Emirates Cargo	Turkish Airlines
Evergreen International	Volga-Dnepr
Finnair	XL Airways Germany
Flybe.	

Hotels

Arabella Sheraton Airport Hotel

Im Flughafen Düsseldorf, 40474 Düsseldorf ☒ +49 21 41 730 ☒ www.sheraton.com
The most convenient hotel at Düsseldorf Airport, and connected to the terminal via a walkway. Rooms on higher floors with numbers ending in 10 will give views of the domestic ramp and distant taxiway. Rooms can be expensive, however.

Holiday Inn Düsseldorf Airport-Ratingen

Broichhofstrasse 3, 40880 Ratingen ☒ +49 21 02 45 60
www.duesseldorf-airport-holiday-inn.de
Affordable option located on the airport's eastern boundary close to the intersection of the A44 and A52 Autobahns. Views of aircraft are too distant to be of use, however users of an SBS may have more luck.

Frankfurt (Main)
Germany

FRA | EDDF

Tel: +49 69 69 00
Web: www.airportcity-frankfurt.com
Passengers: 54.1 million (2007)

Overview

Germany's busiest airport, and one of the busiest in Europe, Frankfurt has been a favourite with aircraft enthusiasts for many years, particularly due to the exotic mix of airliners from the all around the world, eastern Europe, and the military transports using the USAF Rhine-Main base on the south side of the airport.

Scheduled services began on the current airport site in 1936 after an existing airport at nearby Rebstock became overcrowded. The new Rhine-Main airport was also built as an Airship Port, and its first movements - in May 1936 - were the airships Hindenberg and Graf Zeppelin. Deutsche Lufthansa began services to the airport in July 1936 using Junkers Ju52 aircraft.

After the war, the Allied forces oversaw the reconstruction of the airport, allowing commercial flights to begin again on 14 August 1946. A second parallel runway was constructed in 1949 and the airport was handed over to German control. The south side of the airport was, however, retained for military operations, a significant amount of which was by USAF aircraft.

Terminal 2 was opened in 1994, easing congestion at the original terminal complex, which now became Terminal 1 handling all Lufthansa and associated airlines. A new terminal and fourth runway are now in the pipeline, expected to be completed by 2015. The new terminal will occupy the site of the former air base, which vacated the site in 2005.

As well as most of the Lufthansa and Condor fleets, Frankfurt is served by airlines from around the world. It is also one of the few places left to see Russian-built airliners in abundance, which serve various eastern European destinations. There are very few low-cost carriers here.

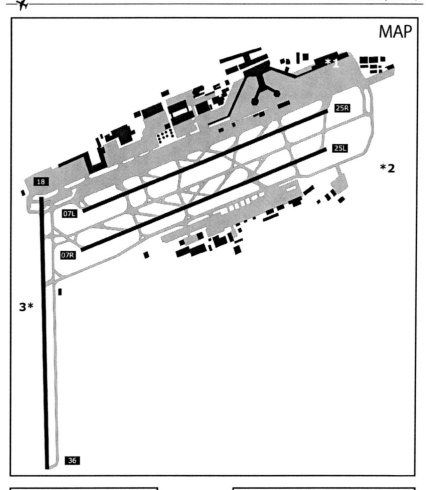

MAP

Frequencies

119.900	Tower
124.850	Tower
118.450	Arrivals
120.800	Arrivals
125.350	Arrivals
120.150	Departures
120.425	Departures
121.700	Apron
121.850	Apron
121.950	Apron
121.800	Ground
127.275	Director
121.900	Delivery
118.025	ATIS
118.725	ATIS

Runways

07R/25L	13,123x148ft / 4,000x45m
07L/25R	13,123x197ft / 4,000x60m
18/36	13,123x148ft / 4,000x45m

Resident Airframes

N87982 Convair 240 Terminal 1 roof, nose only
5A-DGK DC-8-21 Terminal 1 roof, nose only
D-HAUD Sikorsky S-58 Terminal 1 roof
D-ANAF Viscount Lufthansa Training
N88887 DC-4/C-54 Airlift Memorial
43-49081 DC-3/C-47 Airlift Memorial

Spotting Locations

1. Visitors' Terrace

The famous viewing terrace atop Terminal 1 remains closed after building work encroached. The terrace on Terminal 2 was reopened, however. This gives close-up views of the action around this terminal, and the nearby runways and commuter ramp. It can be difficult to see movements at parts of Terminal 1 and Runway 18 from here. Opening times: daily from 10am to 5pm. Last entrance 4.30pm. Adults €4; Concessions €2.50.

2. Autobahn Bridge/Airlift Memorial

From Terminal 2, it is possible to walk past the end of Runways 25L/R along a designated footpath. At ground level outside the terminal, follow Hugo-Eckener-Ring past the catering and office buildings. The footpath starts on the left, crossing a small bridge. Eventually the footpath rises to meet a bridge crossing the Autobahn 5. From here, excellent photographs of aircraft on short finals can be taken, and many movements logged with good binoculars. A little further on is the Berlin Airlift Memorial, with a preserved C-47 and C-54 on display.

3. Runway 18

Runway 18 is north-south facing, and used primarily for departures. A viewing area and small car park was put here to cater for enthusiasts. It is perfect for photographing departures on Runway 18, and also aircraft on short finals for Runways 07L/R. Some aircraft on the taxiways and cargo ramps can be logged from here. Some bus services pass here from Terminal 1.

Airside Spotting

Once airside in both terminals, there are windows around the departure areas which offer limited views of the stands and parallel runways. It is useful to note that information screens scattered around the terminals, both landside and airside, will show aircraft registrations. Look for the 'i' signs.

Hotels

InterCity Hotel Frankfurt Airport

CargoCitySüd,60549Frankfurt ☒ +4969697099 ☒ www.frankfurt-airport.intercityhotel.de

Located on the south side, close to the old USAF base. This hotel has some rooms offering limited views of the parallel runways. TV screens in the lobby often have aircraft registrations listed alongside movements. Short walk to Autobahn Bridge spot.

NH Frankfurt Airport Hotel

Mörfelder Strasse 113, 65451 Frankfurt ☒ +49 61 07 93 80 ☒ www.nh-hotels.com

Affordable hotel, located less than 2km from the terminals, with free shuttles. It is also located a short distance from the Runway 18 spot.

Steigenberger Airport Hotel

Unterschweinstiege 16,60549Frankfurt ☒ +496969750 ☒ www.airporthotel.steigenberger.de

Large, smart hotel located a short distance from the terminals. Slightly pricier, however some rooms and corridors offer limited views of the parallel runways and Terminal 2 ramp.

Airlines

Adria Airways	Bulgarian Air Charter	Iberia	Rossiya
Aegean Airlines	Cargolux	Icelandair	Royal Air Maroc
Aer Lingus	Carpatair	Inter Airlines	Royal Jordanian
Aeroflot	Cathay Pacific	Iran Air	S7 Airlines
Aeroflot-Don	China Airlines	Japan Airlines	Saravia
airberlin	ChinaEasternAirlines	Jat Airways	SAS
Air Algérie	Cirrus Airlines	KLM	SATA Internacional
Air Astana	Clickair	Korean Air	Saudi Arabian Airlines
Air Canada	Condor	Kras Air	Singapore Airlines
Air China	Continental Airlines	KTHY	Singapore Airlines Cargo
Air France	Croatia Airlnes	Kuban Airlines	Sky Airlines
Air India	Cyprus Airways	Kuwait Airways	Spanair
Air Malta	Czech Airlines	LAN Airlines	SriLankan Airlines
Air Mauritius	Delta Air Lines	Libyan Airlines	SunExpress
Air Moldova	DHL Air	LOT Polish Airlines	Swiss International Air Lines
Air Namibia	Dragonair	Lufthansa	Syrian Arab Airlines
Air Seychelles	East Line Airlines	Lufthansa Cargo	TAM
Air Transat	Egyptair	Luxair	TAP Portugal
Air Via	El Al	Malaysia Airlines	TAROM
Albanian Airlines	Emirates	MalévHungarianAirlines	Thai Airways International
Alitalia	Eritrean Airlines	MEAMiddleEastAirlines	Transaero
All Nippon Airways	Estonian Air	Montenegro Airlines	Tunisair
American Airlines	Ethiopian Airlines	Niki	TUIfly.com
Ariana Afghan Airlines	Etihad Airways	Nippon Cargo Airlines	Turkish Airlines
Asiana Airlines	FedEx Express	Northwest Airlines	Turkmenistan Airlines
Atlas Air	Finnair	Nouvelair	UkraineInternationalAirlines
Austrian Airlines	Flybe.	Olympic Airlines	United Airlines
Belavia	FlyLal	Omskavia	US Airways
Blue Wings	Free Bird Airlines	Pegasus Airlines	Uzbekistan Airways
British Airways	Georgian Airways	Polar Air Cargo	Varig
Brussels Airlines	Gulf Air	Qantas	Vietnam Airlines
Bulgaria Air	HamburgInternational	Qatar Airways	Yemenia

Nearby Attractions

Technik Museum Speyer

Am Technik Museum, 67356 Speyer ☒ +49 6232 67080 ☒ www.technik-museum.de

Only an hour south of Frankfurt, the Technik Museum houses a large collection of aircraft, helicopters, cars, trains and other technical innovations. Highlights include a Lufthansa Boeing 747-200, Antonov AN-22, and DC-3. Open daily 9am to 6pm (7pm at weekends).

Geneva (Cointrin)
Switzerland

GVA | LSGG

Tel: +41 (0) 22 71 77 111
Web: www.gva.ch
Passengers: 10.8 million (2007)

Overview

Geneva's airport is located in the area of Cointrin to the north of the city. A landing strip has existed here since the 1920s, though major expansion was undertaken after World War II, and again in the 1960s to cope with a massive growth in air travel to the city.

The fairly unique system of remote satellites with their own aircraft gates, linked by underground passage to the main terminal, is still in use today allowing good management of the limited space available. Without this, congestion in busy periods would become unmanageable.

Since 1956, an exchange of territory has been agreed with France, whereby the terminal allows passengers destined for France to exit via different channels and ultimately onto the road heading straight to the French border. For departing passengers, a separate area of the terminal has been set aside for those travelling to France. Understandably Air France is the dominant user of this area.

Geneva is very much an international city, with organisations based in the city including the European headquarters of the United Nations. There are also many conferences held in Geneva annually. This all bodes very well for the airport, which as a result handles more business jet movements than most other European airports, and is also high on the list of most European airlines. Additionally during the colder winter months, Geneva plays host to an influx of leisure passengers destined for the nearby ski resorts in the Alps.

MAP

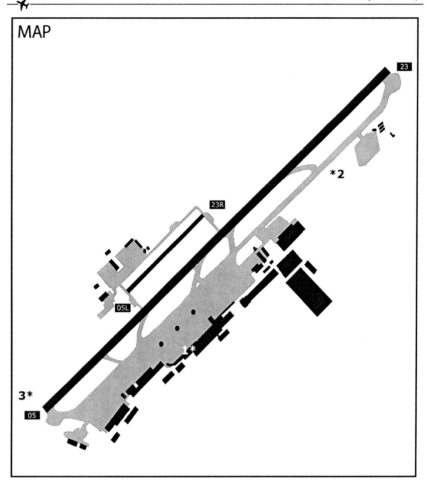

Frequencies

118.700 Tower
119.700 Tower
119.900 Tower
131.325 Approach
136.250 Arrival
120.300 Finals
136.450 Transit
119.525 VFR Traffic
118.700 Ground
119.700 Ground
121.900 Ground
121.175 Ramp
135.570 ATIS

Runways

05/23   12,795x164ft / 3,900x50m
05L/23R 2,700x98ft / 823x30m

Spotting Locations

1. View Point Terrace

The open terrace along the rooftop of the terminal building is an excellent provision by the airport, and is well maintained with seating and a cafe. Views from here extend along the runway in both directions, and most parts of the main ramp can be seen, as well as one of the business jet ramps on the far side of the runway. What can not be seen parked from here can usually be seen as it departs. The terrace is fronted by glass, but this is usually fine for photography. Access is from within the terminal. **NOTE - The View Point Terrace was closed at the time of printing due to construction work on the Terminal.**

2. Runway 23

When aircraft are arriving over the lake, follow the road from the terminal towards Cargo-Fret. After a u-turn to join the highway, go under the Palexpo convention centre in the direction of Ferney. After passing over the highway again, turn left at the lights and then stay to the right. You will see the barracks and an embankment, which offers elevated views over the runway and taxiway. Bus route 28 from the terminal passes this spot in the direction of Jardin Botanique. Get off at Tunnel Routier stop.

3. Runway 05

At the Runway 05 end, leave the terminal and head for Meyrin, past the World Trade Center. Turn right at the lights for Meyrin, and then turn right at the Tag Aviation signpost. After a u-turn, you will pass some buildings before the road turns left. Park in the car park on the right and then walk back in the direction you came from, and down a pedestrian path which leads to a fence near the runway threshold. Bus 28 to Hopital La Tour leaves the terminal in this direction. Alight at Blandonnet and walk towards Tag Aviation and the pedestrian path.

Airside Spotting

Most gate areas, both in the Swiss and French sections of the terminal, have windows through which movements can be logged.

Security

Security at Geneva is of a high level, but the aviation enthusiast is understood completely and you will not be troubled whilst using the viewing terrace for spotting and photography. Occasionally, to coincide with the arrival of an important dignitary, the terrace has been known to close.

Resident Airframes

F-GCJL 737-222 Fire service
HZ-TNA Jetstar

Airlines

Aer Lingus	easyJet Switzerland	Malév Hungarian Airlines
Aeroflot	Edelweiss Air	MEA Middle East Airlines
Afriqiyah Airways	Egyptair	Norwegian Air Shuttle
Air Algérie	El Al	Olympic Airlines
Air Europa	Etihad Airways	Qatar Airways
Air France	Farnair Switzerland	Rossiya
Air India	Finnair	Royal Air Maroc
Air Malta	Flybaboo	Royal Jordanian
Air Mauritius	Flybe.	SAS
Alitalia	FlyGlobespan	Saudi Arabian Airlines
Atlas Blue	Hello	Sterling
Austrian Airlines	Helvetic Airways	Swiss International Air Lines
Blue Islands	Iberia	TAP Portugal
bmibaby	Iran Air	Thai Airways International
British Airways	Jet2	ThomsonFly
Brussels Airlines	KLM	TNT Airways
CityJet	Kuwait Airways	Transavia
Continental Airlines	LOT Polish Airlines	Tunisair
Darwin Airline	Lufthansa	Turkish Airlines
easyJet	Luxair	

Hotels

Crowne Plaza Geneva Airport

34 Route Francoise-Peyrot, Geneva 1218 ☒ +41 22 747 0202 ☒ www.crowneplaza.com
Situated within walking distance of the terminal building. Has very few views of aircraft movements, and can be expensive at certain times of year.

Express by Holiday Inn

Route de Pre-Bois 16, Geneva 1215 ☒ +41 22 93 93 939 ☒ www.holidayinn.com
Situated alongside the major motorway, and also next to one of the business jet ramps. Some of the higher rooms have views of the action. Free shuttle to the terminal.

Mövenpick Hotel Geneva Airport

Route de Pre-Bois 20, Geneva 1215 ☒ +41 22 717 1111 ☒ www.moevenpick-hotels.com
Situated alongside the Holiday Inn, and sometimes more affordable. Again, some higher rooms offer views of aircraft, although these can be limited. Free shuttle to the terminal.

NH Geneva Airport Hotel

Av. De Mategnin 21, Geneva 1217 ☒ +41 22 98 99 000 ☒ www.nh-hotels.com
One of the best-placed hotels at Geneva Airport for the enthusiast. Although not all rooms offer views, the ones that do face the threshold of Runway 05. The hotel is also close to the spotting location at this end of the runway.

Hamburg (Finkenwerder)
Germany

XFW | EDHI
Tel: +49 (0) 40 74 370
Web: www.airbus.com
Passengers: N/A

Overview

Finkenwerder Airport is located in the south west of the city of Hamburg in northern Germany. It is primarily used as a manufacturing and outfitting site by Airbus, in addition to their Toulouse facility in France.

The plant is the third largest aircraft manufacturing facility in the world and employs around 10,000 staff. Airbus A318, A319 and A321 models are manufactured here, as well as sections of the A380 fuselage and wings. Other models are also brought here to have their interiors fitted and final paint schemes applied ready for delivery.

Finkenwerder doesn't have any commercial flights, but regularly handles freighters of all sizes in addition to the A300-600ST "Belugas" operated by Airbus. In addition to this, there are two daily staff flights to Toulouse, and many executive jet movements in relation to Airbus' activities.

Naturally many aircraft enthusiasts visit Finkenwerder to log new airframes, many of which will shortly be flying in far flung corners of the world and not seen again in Europe. A number of spots around the airport offer views and opportunities for photography. It is advised to park your car in one of the two lots near the delivery centre, and walk to the spotting locations. Bus line 150 from Altona station will deliver you close by if you alight at Neß-Hauptdeich.

MAP

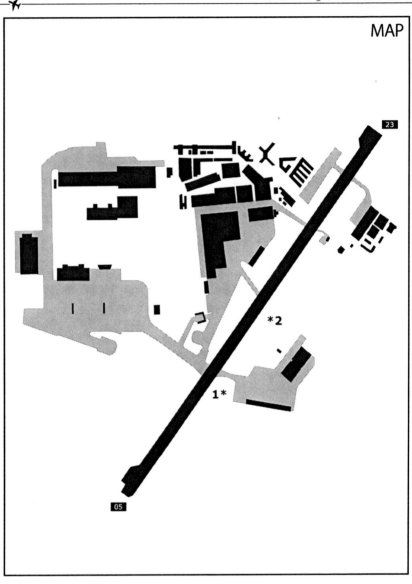

23

*2

1*

05

Frequencies

123.250 Tower

Runways

05/23   8,629x148ft / 2,630x45m

Spotting Locations

1. Road Crossing

The most famous spot at Finkenwerder is the point where the taxiway crosses the road. Cars must stop to let aircraft cross. Standing near the dike at this point gives you close access for photographs as aircraft pass to and from the delivery centre.

2. The Dike

The dike running the length of the runway gives good views of aircraft landing and departing. It is good for photographs until late afternoon, and most aircraft parked in the open can be logged from here.

Nearby Attractions

Hamburg Fuhlsbüttel Airport

Hamburg's main airport handles flights across German, Europe and many far away destinations. It is one of Germany's busier airports and naturally handles a lot of Germany's airline operators. There are official viewing decks at each terminal and various locations around the perimeter.

Hotels

Hotel Kiek-in Garni

Nordmeerstraße 48, 21129 Hamburg ☒ +45 (0) 40 74 21 550 ☒ www.hotel-kiek-in.de

A small and affordable hotel in a residential district very close to the delivery centre at Finkenwerder. There are no views of aircraft from the hotel, but it is very convenient.

InterCity Hotel

Paul-Nevermann-Platz 17, 22765 Hamburg ☒ +49 (0) 40 38 03 40
www.hamburg-altona.intercityhotel.de

If you choose to stay in Hamburg itself, the InterCity is a modern and affordable option outside Altona station. This is easily accessible by car and bus from Finkenwerder, and also Hamburg's main airport.

Helsinki (Vantaa)
Finland

HEL | EFHK

Tel: +358 20 01 46 36

Web: www.helsinki-vantaa.fi

Passengers: 13.1 million (2007)

Overview

Finland has always had a strong association with aviation. The capital, Helsinki, is today a fairly busy hub for the national carrier and handles a number of flights from across Europe, North America, the Middle and Far East. In addition to this, a healthy cargo operation takes place at the airport.

The airport at Vantaa was opened in 1952 for the Helsinki Olympics. It replaced the older facility at Malmi, which today is used as the city's general aviation airport. A number of expansion projects are underway at Vantaa to help the airport cope with future growth.

The weather can often put a dampener on spending time at Helsinki, but long hours of sunlight in the summer months also prove advantageous. When the weather is against you, the café in the International Terminal provides a warm location with excellent views.

Whilst most of Europe's airlines visit Helsinki, its proximity to former Soviet and Baltic states means there's always something of interest passing through. Runway 22L is the most commonly used for movements due to the prevalent winds and noise abatement procedures, however runways can regularly be switched or used in parallel.

MAP

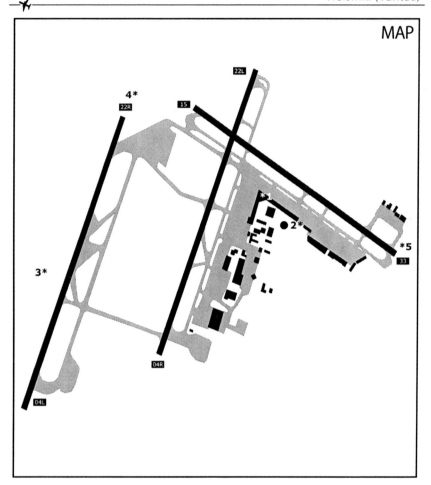

Frequencies

118.600	Tower
119.100	Radar
129.850	Radar
119.100	Approach
119.700	Approach
119.900	Arrivals
118.125	Clearance
121.800	Ground
114.200	ATIS Departures
135.075	ATIS

Runways

04R/22L	11,286x197ft / 3,440x60m
04L/22R	10,039x197ft / 3,060x60m
15/33	9,518x197ft / 2,901x60m

Spotting Locations

1. International Terminal Café

Located between halls 2 and 3 on the 3rd floor of the International Terminal (another café on the 2nd floor also has some views). The café has large windows fronting the aprons and the taxiways and runways. Most of the traffic will pass here at some point. Photography is possible, however the glass is usually dirty.

2. Domestic Terminal

Outside the Domestic Terminal, walk to the right for 100m until you reach the ramp which allows you views over the movements. This is the best spot when runways 15 or 33 are in use, as traffic will taxi past you on the way in and out. Be warned that aircraft can park in front of you, rendering the spot of little use. Some views of the cargo apron and passenger gates are possible from here.

3. Runway 04L/22R

Exit the terminal area along Lentoasemantie and turn right at the traffic lights. Around 3km later, turn right at a T-junction and drive along Katriinantie until the runway comes into view. Try any of the gravel roads on the right. There are various spots along here which can lead to fantastic photographs when the runway is in use. Some sand hills give you an elevated view, but bring a ladder if you have one.

4. Runway 15

Exit the terminal area along Lentoasemantie and turn right at the traffic lights. Around 3km later, turn right at a T-junction and drive along Katriinantie, then follow sign Myllykylä/Kvarnbacken. Drive for 500m and turn right next to a billboard. Drive for 800m and turn right. Leave your car near the junction and walk to the left past a hill. This elevated spot gives great photos of aircraft on short finals to Runway 15.

5. Runway 33

Exit the terminal towards Kehä/Ring III, then take the first exit and turn left at the lights towards RAHTI. Then turn left towards RAHTI II. Turn left after 900m, passing the TNT building. Turn left at the T-junction and then park. The sand hills here have an elevated position with views over Runway 15/33 and the cargo ramps. Photography is possible of aircraft parked here, as well as those on the runway and taxiway. The sun can be a problem from late morning.

Airside Spotting

Once airside, large windows can be found alongside most gates at Helsinki. Conditions are not perfect for photography, however most movements can be logged.

Airlines

Aer Lingus	Finnair
Aeroflot	Finncomm Airlines
airberlin	Fly Lappeenranta
airest	Icelandair
Air Åland	KLM
Air Finland	Korean Air Cargo
airBaltic	LOT Polish Airlines
Austrian Airlines	Lufthansa
Avies	Malév Hungarian Airlines
Blue1	Rossiya
British Airways	SAS
Brussels Airlines	Skyways
Cargolux	TNT Airways
Cimber Air	Turkish Airlines
Czech Airlines	Ukraine International Airlines
DHL Air	UPS
Estonian Air	West Air Sweden

Hotels

Hilton Helsinki-Vantaa Airport

Lentajankuja 1, Vantaa 01530 ☒ +358 97 32 22 211 ☒ www.hilton.com

Situated at the terminal complex. Expensive hotel, but some higher rooms have views of aircraft movements.

Cumulus Airport Hotel

Robert Huberin Tie 4, Vantaa 01510 ☒ +358 94 15 77 100

No reports of any rooms with views of movements, however the hotel has a number of floors and is only a short distance from the terminal area and the threshold of Runway 04R, so there is a possibility. The benefit of this hotel is that it's one of the more affordable at Vantaa.

Nearby Attractions

Finnish Aviation Museum

Helsinki-Vantaa Airport, Tietotie 3, Vantaa 01539
+358 98 70 08 70 ☒ www.suomenilumuseo.fi

This popular museum houses over 70 historic aircraft linked in some way to Finnish aviation history. Included are a Convair 440, DC-2 and a DC-3. It is open daily from 11am to 6pm. Adults E6, Children/Concessions E3.

Helsinki Malmi Airport

Malmi Airport is the original Helsinki Airport. It has a well-preserved pre-war terminal building. Malmi is the city's general aviation airport. Ramp access can occasionally be granted, otherwise views are possible from the terminal area.

Lisbon (Portela)
Portugal

LIS | LPPT
Tel: +35 12 18 41 26 75
Web: www.ana.pt
Passengers: 13.4 million (2007)

Overview

Although one of Europe's quietest capitals, a trip to Lisbon can still yield a number of exotic aircraft, and the opportunity to spot in the sun is never to be scoffed at.

Relatively few spotters make the journey to Lisbon, unless special events are being held in the city. Most prefer the more commonly visited Faro airport on the popular Algarve coast to the south.

Flying directly to Lisbon is an option with most European airlines, and a number of long haul carriers from North and South America, and Africa. Alternatively, the drive from the Algarve is less than three hours.

One word of warning regarding Lisbon's airport is that the government finally announced in 2006 that it has picked a location for a replacement airport. This is to be at Alcochete to the north of the city, on the site of the current military airfield there. This will likely happen by 2015 at the earliest.

In the meantime the current airport, which is hemmed in by motorways and buildings, struggles to cope with the movements and passenger numbers. It has recently opened the modern Terminal 2, and in recent years, a Boeing 707 which had been stored for many years was scrapped to create more space.

Lisbon is the main operating base of Portuguese national carrier TAP, as well as PGA Portugalia, Sata International, and EuroAtlantic. A number of low-fare carriers now operate into Lisbon.

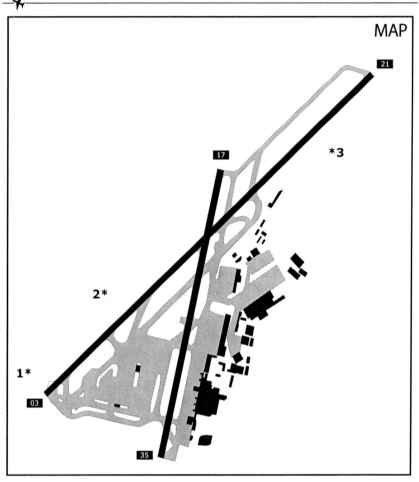

MAP

Frequencies

118.100 Tower
118.950 Tower
119.100 Approach
118.950 Ground
121.750 Ground
124.150 ATIS

Runways

03/21   12,484x148ft / 3,805x45m
17/35   7,874x148ft / 2,400x45m

Spotting Locations

1. Calvanas

This is the most popular spot to watch and photograph aircraft at Lisbon. It includes a small hill overlooking the threshold of Runway 03, with unobstructed views and perfect sunlight all afternoon. It is not really suitable when the Runway 21 direction is in use. To drive there, take the Camarate/Charneca/Alvalade exit from the south/westbound E01 motorway, then take the first right and find somewhere to park near the houses. Alternatively Bus 17 will drop you at Calvanas if you ask the driver. Building work in the near future may render this location unusable. There are snack bars close by.

2. Runway 03/21

Half-way along Runway 03/21 is another spot which can offer good photography, and an overview of all the airport's movements, and aircraft parked on the various ramps. To reach the spot, follow directions to location 1, but continue along the road after leaving the motorway at Camarate/Charneca/Alvalade. Take the 2nd exit at the roundabout and continue.

3. Raised Area

Walking from the terminal along the approach road, you will come to a busy roundabout. Take the first exit on the left and follow the footpath up the hill, with a small football pitch nearby. From here, aircraft using the runway and taxiways can be observed, and aircraft on the remote stands can be logged. A good spot for photography.

Airside Spotting

Mesh on the windows once airside make spotting very difficult, diffusing the light. General movements can be observed, but photography is impossible and accurate reading is difficult.

Security

Aircraft spotting is understood and accepted by the authorities. Be careful not to trespass on any airport property.

Resident Airframes

CS-TDA Douglas DC-3 Preserved

Airlines

Aerocondor	EuroAtlantic Airways	SATA Internacional
Aer Lingus	Eurocypria Airlines	SkyEurope
Aigle Azur	FedEx Express	Skyservice
airberlin	Finnair	Star Air
Air Cairo	Flyant	SunExpress
Air Comet	Futura	Swiftair
Air Europa	Germanwings	Swiss International Air Lines
Air France	Hemus Air	TAAG Angola Airlines
Air Moldova	Iberia	TAER Andalus
Air Nostrum	Iberworld	TACV Cabo Verde
Air Transat	Karthago Airlines	TAP Portugal
Alitalia	KLM	TNT Airways
Axis Airways	KrasAir	Transavia
Blue Air	Livingston Airlines	Travel Service
bmibaby	Lufthansa	Tunisair
British Airways	Luzair	Turkish Airlines
Brussels Airlines	Lviv Airlines	Ukraine International Airlines
Centralwings	MNG Airlines	UPS
Clickair	Niki	US Airways
Continental Airlines	Nouvelair	Varig Log
DHL Airways	Orbest	Viking Airlines
Dubrovnik Airline	Portugalia	Vueling
easyJet	Regional Air Lines	White
easyJet Switzerland	Royal Air Maroc	Windjet
Egyptair	SAS	

Hotels

Radisson SAS Lisbon Airport

390 Avenue Marechal Craveiro Lopes, Lisbon 1749-009
+351 (21) 004 5000 ⊠ www.lisbon.radissonsas.com

The only hotel at Lisbon with any aircraft views. Even numbered rooms on the 10th floor yield the best results. Hotel is fairly expensive.

London (Gatwick)
United Kingdom

LGW | EGKK

Tel: +44 (0) 87 00 00 24 68

Web: www.gatwickairport.co.uk

Passengers: 35.16 million (2007)

Overview

Gatwick is London's second largest airport, and situated to the south of the city. It is the London airport where many of the country's charter and low-cost carriers operate, as well as some of the larger airlines from around the world. Due to the recent Open Skies arrangement, a number of the North American airlines relegated to Gatwick have been given access to the more lucrative Heathrow airport. Where this will leave Gatwick is not known yet.

British Airways retains a healthy presence at Gatwick, operating short, medium and long haul services with a dedicated fleet that will not usually be seen on an average visit to Heathrow.

Gatwick has two terminals – North and South. It is the world's busiest single runway airport. This can lead to lengthy delays and some spectacularly short gaps between departing and arriving traffic.

Sadly Gatwick also fell foul of the British Airports Authority (BAA) when they got rid of the excellent viewing terrace on the South Terminal in favour of expansion. This left Gatwick with no official viewing facilities. It has since proved a very frustrating airport for the enthusiast.

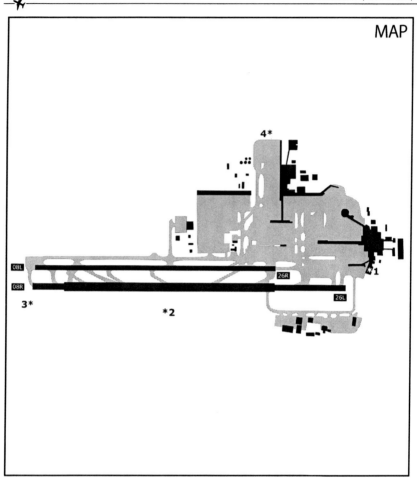

MAP

Frequencies

124.225 Tower
134.225 Tower
126.825 Approach
121.800 Ground
121.950 Clearance Delivery
118.950 Director
135.575 Director
128.475 ATIS
136.525 ATIS

Runways

08R/26L 10,364x148ft / 3,159x45m
08L/26R 8,415x148ft / 2,565x45m

Spotting Locations

1. Multi-Storey Car Park

The top level of the Multi-Storey car park at the southern end of the South Terminal is a nice spot for logging aircraft on the southern pier, and aircraft on short finals to Runway 26L. Facing into the sun is not ideal, however. Signs at this location indicate that spotters are not welcome to loiter.

2. Southern Perimeter Road

Following the perimeter road south and then west from the South Terminal opens up a number of opportunities to see aircraft on the runway. There are limited places to park a car along here. Be careful not to block any crash gates or entrances. Photography is possible in places.

3. Runway 08R

Following Charlwood Road and Lowfield Heath Road around the end of Runway 08R also brings a few opportunities to park up and photograph or log aircraft on short finals or lining up on this runway. This is the most popular spot for spotters these days.

4. Perimeter Road North

The Perimeter Road North runs to the car parks for the North Terminal. It passes the apron where most aircraft using this terminal are parked, and is therefore worth a stop to log what can be seen. Not of use for photography.

Airside Spotting

Both terminals have opportunities in all airside areas for spotting movements – much better than any other facilities! In the North Terminal, the impressive bridge linking the main building with the satellite pier gives fantastic aerial views over the aprons, including aircraft passing beneath you.

Resident Airframes

G-CEXP HP Herald Stored

Nearby Attractions

Gatwick Aviation Museum

Lowfield Heath Road, Gatwick, Surrey RH6 0BT
+44 (0) 12 93 86 29 15 ☒ www.gatwick-aviation-museum.co.uk

A collection of preserved historic aircraft can be found a mile or so north of the Runway 08R threshold. Mostly military and wartime aircraft. Check the website or call for opening days.

Airlines

Adria Airways	Croatia Airlines	Norwegian Air Shuttle
Aer Lingus	Cubana	Nouvelair
African Safari Airways	Daallo Airlines	Oasis Hong Kong
Afriqiyah Airways	Delta Air Lines	Oman Air
airBaltic	easyJet	Onur Air
Air Comet	easyJet Switzerland	Qatar Airways
Air Malta	Emirates	Rossiya
Air Namibia	Estonian Air	Ryanair
Air Southwest	Eurocypria Airlines	SAS
Air Transat	First Choice Airways	Safi Airways
Air Zimbabwe	Flybe.	SATA Internacional
American Airlines	FlyLal	Sterling
Astraeus	Free Bird Airlines	TAP Portugal
Atlas Blue	Ghana International Airlines	TAROM
Aurigny Air Services	Karthago Airlines	Thomas Cook Airlines
Azerbaijan Airlines	KD-Avia	ThomsonFly
Belavia	KTHY	Ukraine International Airlines
BH Air	LTE International Airways	US Airways
British Airways	Malaysia Airlines	Virgin Atlantic
Brussels Airlines	Malév Hungarian Airlines	Virgin Nigeria
Bulgaria Air	Meridiana	Wizz Air
Centralwings	Monarch Airlines	XL Airways
Clickair	Nationwide Airlines	Zoom Airlines
Continental Airlines	Northwest Airlines	Zoom Airlines UK

Hotels

Sofitel London Gatwick Airport

North Terminal, Gatwick Airport RH6 0PH ☒ +44 (0) 1293 567070 ☒ www.sofitel.com
Smart hotel situated at the North Terminal, and linked via monorail from the South
Terminal. Rooms on the higher floors facing the airport have unrivalled views of air-
craft movements to both terminals. Expensive.

Travelodge Gatwick Airport

Church Road, Lowfield Heath, Crawley RH11 0PQ
+44 (0) 87 19 84 60 31 ☒ www.travelodge.co.uk
Although its rooms don't offer any realistic views of the airport, it is situated a stone's
throw from the southern perimeter, and therefore perfect for the only useful spotting
locations. It is a more affordable hotel.

London (Heathrow)
United Kingdom

LHR | EGLL

Tel: +44 (0) 87 00 00 01 23
Web: www.heathrowairport.co.uk
Passengers: 67.8 million (2007)

Overview

One of the biggest crimes to the spotting community in the United Kingdom of recent years has been the removal of the viewing facilities at Heathrow and Gatwick airports. The terraces above the Queen's Building and Terminal 2 at Heathrow were excellent, allowing photography and logging of all movements.

Since the changes, which came about when expansion and terrorist threats became priority, spotters have had to find alternatives around the airport. All is not lost, however, as photography and logging is still possible.

Heathrow airport is Europe's busiest and very overcrowded. The variety of airlines operating here is mouth-watering to the enthusiast, and come from all corners of the globe. It is the operating and maintenance base for British Airways and Virgin Atlantic. The recently-announced Open Skies agreement has also attracted a number of new carriers to the airport which were previously relegated to Gatwick and other airports.

Heathrow has a two parallel runways, 09L/27R and 09R/27L. The former cross runway 23/05 is no longer used other than as a taxiway. Patterns of runway assignment between landing and departing usually switch during the day.

In the central area you'll find terminals 1, 2, and 3. Terminal 4 is located to the south east of the runways, and the new Terminal 5 is to the west of the central area. Runway 09L/27R is 3,902m (12,800ft) and 09R/27L is 3,658m (12,000ft).

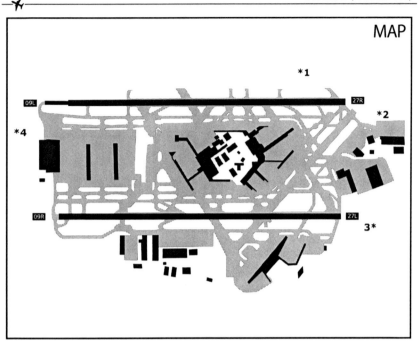

MAP

Frequencies

118.500	Tower South 27L/09R
118.700	Tower North 27R/09L
124.475	Tower
119.900	Radar
118.825	Arrivals/DeparturesNortheast
119.775	Arrivals/DeparturesNorthwest
120.525	Arrivals/DeparturesSoutheast
133.175	Arrivals/DeparturesSouthwest
134.125	Arrivals/DeparturesSouthwest
134.750	Departures Compton
134.975	Arrivals Ockham
125.625	Approach
135.125	Approach
135.325	Departures South
121.700	Ground South
121.850	Ground
121.900	Ground North
124.475	Ground
121.975	Clearance Delivery
120.400	Director
121.935	ATIS Departures
128.075	ATIS
133.075	ATIS

Runways

09R/27L 12,001x148ft / 3,658x45m
09L/27R 12,799x164m / 3,901x50m

Spotting Locations

1. Heathrow Academy

Formerly the Visitor Centre. When the viewing facilities on the Queen's Building closed, this became the only official spotting location. The Academy can be found on Newall Road, off the Northern Perimeter Road. It houses a café, hobby shop, exhibition and classroom facilities. A grandstand has recently been erected outside the Academy for the viewing of aircraft movements. It is not of much use for photography, but plenty of movements can be logged. The Academy is open from 10am to 4pm on weekends and school holidays.

2. Runway 27R

Following the Northern Perimeter Road past the Academy will take you under the approach to Runway 27R. There are some places to park along the side of the road, however buses run regularly along this route from the terminals and hotels. Excellent for photography when this runway is in use for arrivals.

3. Runway 27L / Hatton Cross Underground

Follow the Eastern Perimeter Road until you reach Hatton Cross Underground station. From here, spots under the approach for Runway 27L are perfect for photography. Some views of aircraft in the central terminal area, as well as Terminal 4 and the maintenance hangars are possible from here. It is best to walk from Hatton Cross rather than risk parking the car at the side of the road.

4. Runways 09L/R

Running the length of the western perimeter is Stanwell Moor Road. You will often find cars parked along the verge here when this runway direction is in use. It is better for Runway 09L, although walking south will yield results for 09R. Photography is good. The opening of Terminal 5 may limit the use of this spot.

Airside Spotting

Terminals 1, 2 and 4 have plenty of airside windows with views of aircraft manoeuvring around the airport and parked at gates. Terminal 3 is very limited in its views, apart from some departure lounges in the pier. Terminal 5 is one of the best for airside spotting, with large windows at either end of the main building and Pier B overlooking the runway thresholds.

Nearby Attractions

Brooklands Museum

Weybridge, Surrey KT130QN ⌧ +44(0)1932855465 ⌧ www.brooklandsmuseum.com

The former racing circuit and airfield was the production site for most Vickers aircraft for many years. Today the site is largely used by Mercedes-Benz for testing, however a museum in one corner has an excellent collection of historic buildings and aircraft built at the site. These include Vickers Viscount, VC-10s, Varsity, Vanguard, a Concorde prototype and many more. The museum also covers the famous racing circuit.

Airlines

Aer Lingus	Blue1	Icelandair	Royal Air Maroc
Aeroflot	bmi	Iran Air	Royal Brunei Airlines
Air Algérie	British Airways	Japan Airlines	Royal Jordanian
Air Astana	Cargolux	Jat Airways	SAS
Air Canada	Cathay Pacific	Jet Airways	Saudi Arabian Airlines
Air China	ChinaEasternAirlines	Kenya Airways	Singapore Airlines
Air France	ChinaSouthernAirlines	KLM	South African Airways
Air India	Clickair	Korean Air	SriLankan Airlines
Air Malta	Continental Airlines	KTHY	Sudan Airways
Air Mauritius	Croatia Airlines	Kuwait Airways	Swiss Air Lines
Air New Zealand	Cyprus Airways	Libyan Airlines	Syrian Arab Airlines
Air Seychelles	Czech Airlines	LOT Polish Airlines	TAM
Air Transat	Delta Air Lines	Lufthansa	TAP Portugal
Alitalia	DHL Airways	Luxair	TAROM
All Nippon Airways	Egyptair	Malaysia Airlines	Thai Airways Int'l
American Airlines	El Al	MEAMiddleEastAirlines	Transaero
Asiana Airlines	Emirates	Northwest Airlines	Tunisair
Atlas Air	Ethiopian Airlines	Nouvelair	Turkish Airlines
Atlas Blue	Etihad Airways	Olympic Airlines	Turkmenistan Airlines
Austrian Airlines	EVA Air	PIAPakistanInt.Airlines	United Airlines
Azerbaijan Airlines	Finnair	Polar Air Cargo	US Airways
Bellview Airlines	Gulf Air	Qantas	Uzbekistan Airways
Bestair	Hemus Air	Qatar Airways	Virgin Atlantic
Biman Bangladesh	Iberia	Rossiya	Yemenia

Resident Airframes

G-BOAB Concorde British Airways Stored

Hotels

Renaissance London Heathrow

140 Bath Road, Hounslow TW6 2AQ ✆ +44 (0) 20 88 97 63 63 ⌨ www.marriott.com

This is one of the best spotting hotels in the world, if you request a room overlooking the airport. All movements on the northern runway can be read off and photographed easily. Movements around the terminals are easy to spot. Those using SBS can continue to spot throughout the night. Although this hotel is not the cheapest at Heathrow, the quality of spotting makes up for it.

Holiday Inn London Heathrow Ariel

118 Bath Road, Harlington, Hayes UB3 5AJ ✆ +44 (0) 20 8990 0000 ⌨ www.holidayinn.com

Another good spotting hotel at Heathrow. Even-numbered rooms between 270 and 284 have the best views of aircraft using the northern runway and terminal areas. Photography is possible. The hotel is slightly cheaper than the Renaissance.

London (Luton)
United Kingdom

LTN | EGGW

Tel: +44 (0)1582 405100
Web: www.london-luton.co.uk
Passengers: 9.94 million (2007)

Overview

Luton is London's fourth largest airport, and is situated some 30 miles north on the main M1 motorway linking the capital with the north of the country. It opened in 1938 and served as an air base in the Second World War.

Today the airport is a busy gateway for low cost carriers and holiday charter airlines. It is the home base of easyJet, ThomsonFly and Monarch Airlines. Ryanair also has a large presence at the airport. A small number of cargo airlines also pass through each day.

Luton is perhaps best known amongst enthusiasts for the large variety of business jets which pass through on a regular basis. The airport has many ramps and hangars dedicated to this traffic.

Despite its size and importance, Luton has quite a cramped and confusing central area which includes the terminals, car parks, roads and administration buildings. You will see signs around this area discouraging spotters from stopping. It is possible to do a quick stop and log in order to catch some aircraft not visible from anywhere else. It is better, however, to use one of the accepted places for watching aircraft.

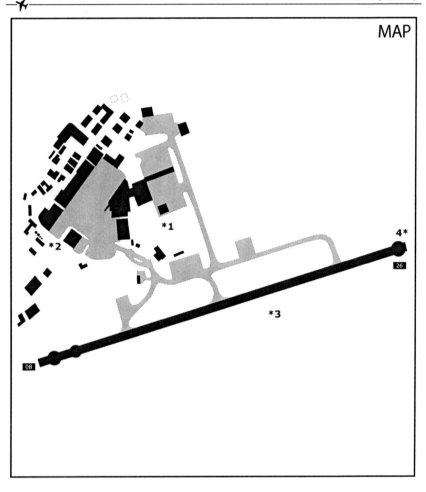

MAP

*1

*2

4*

26

*3

08

Frequencies

126.725 Tower
132.550 Tower
129.550 Approach
128.750 Director
121.750 Ground
120.575 ATIS

Runways

08/26   7,086x151ft / 2,160x46m

Spotting Locations

1. Terminal Building & Car Park

Inside the passenger terminal there are limited views of the main apron and taxiway without actually going airside. The Short Stay Car Park alongside the terminal is also a good place to log some of the aircraft parked at the gates and remote stands.

2. Central Area

Driving around the access roads to the hangars, cargo centre and other parts of the central complex will offer glimpses of many business jets and other aircraft parked around the various aprons. Signs discourage spotters from parking in these areas, so make only quick stops to log what you can see.

3. Crash Gate

Head away from the terminal area towards the M1. Turn right at the second roundabout and then right again towards Wheathamstead. After a couple of miles, turn left at a crossroads, under a railway bridge and up the hill. Turn left at the next junction and keep right. Turn left at the houses, and park alongside the road when it reaches the fence. Keep the crash gate clear at all times! Views of aircraft using the runway are good from here, and photography is possible.

4. Runway 26

Follow directions for the Crash Gate spot (above), but turn right at the houses. Then take the first left. The road will pass very close to the end of Runway 26. Excellent photographs of aircraft on short finals can be taken here, although parking is a problem.

Airside

Windows airside do offer some views of aircraft parked around you, but due to the layout of the airport and terminal buildings, it will never be possible to see everything. It is certainly difficult to log aircraft on the executive ramps from the terminal.

Resident Airframes

G-AOVS Bristol Britannia, fire dump

Websites

http://www.freewebs.com/lutonspotters

Airlines

Aer Arann

Air Atlantic

DHL Air

easyJet

Flybe.

MNG Airlines

Monarch Airlines

Onur Air

Ryanair

SkyEurope

Thomas Cook Airlines

ThomsonFly

Wizz Air

XL Airways

Hotels

Holiday Inn Express Luton Airport

2 Percival Way, Luton LU2 9GP ⊠ +44 (0) 1582 58 91 00 ⊠ www.hiexpress.com

Rooms facing the airport are all great for logging aircraft, and also have plenty of opportunities for good photographs. The hotel is relatively cheap.

Ibis Hotel Premier Travel Inn Luton Airport

Osborne Road, Luton LU1 3HJ ⊠ +44 (0) 8701 97 71 66 ⊠ www.premierinn.com

A comfortable and affordable travel inn located under the approach to Runway 08. Aircraft viewing opportunities will be very minimal, but the central terminal area is very close to the hotel.

London (Stansted)
United Kingdom

STN | EGSS

Tel: +44 (0) 87 00 00 03 03
Web: www.stanstedairport.co.uk
Passengers: 23.7 million (2007)

Overview

Stansted is a busy airport 30 miles north east of London which has seen dramatic growth since the early 1990s when the impressive single terminal building, designed by Sir Norman Foster, was opened to replace the inadequate facilities on the original site.

The airport had started life as a bomber base and maintenance depot in the Second World War. The potential for passenger operations were realised when the British Airports Authority (BAA) took over in 1966.

When low-cost airlines Ryanair, Go and Buzz needed cheaper access to London, Stansted was chosen, and it quickly grew to handle the demand. Go was quickly swallowed by easyJet, and Buzz by Ryanair, leaving these two airlines as the main operators. Today number of other low-cost airlines also have a large presence at Stansted, including Air Berlin and Germanwings.

A number of charter, long-haul and cargo airlines can also be found operating through Stansted on a daily basis.

Stansted has a single runway, though it is expected another is to be built in the next decade to cope with the increased strain on the airport.

Sadly no official viewing locations were ever provided, and watching the action can be difficult if you're not catching a flight.

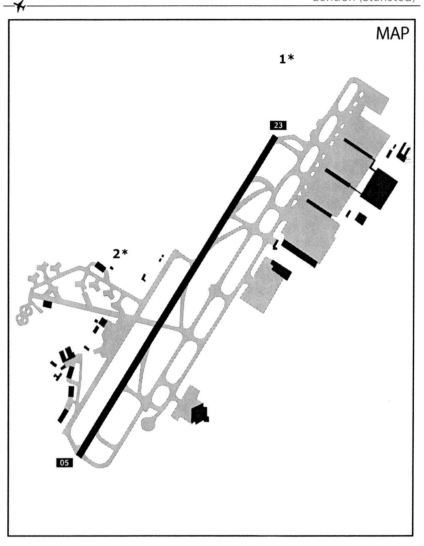

MAP

Frequencies

123.800 Tower
121.950 Clearance Delivery
121.950 Ground
120.625 Director
126.950 Director
127.175 ATIS

Runways

05/23   10,000x150ft / 3,048x46m

Spotting Locations

1. Runway 23

At the end of Runway 23 is a field from which aircraft on short final can be photographed and logged. It is of no use for watching ground movements as a hill is in the way. To reach this spot, take the road past the terminal, but continue to Molehill Green and Elsenham. Go past Molehill Green and take a left at a technology factor along Green Street. Park your car at the end and walk into the field.

2. Old Terminal Area

On the opposite side of the airport close to the Runway 05 end is the old terminal area, now used for maintenance, executive jets, and aircraft storage. There are a number of old aircraft that have been stored here for years, and on any day there are likely to be some exotic business jets present. From the airport exit from the M11, take the 2nd exit at the roundabout instead of heading to the Terminal. This leads to the Long Stay Car Parks. Bypass these and follow Round Coppice Road, turning into Bury Lodge Lane. After passing the village of Burton End, look out for places to pull up on the right and log what you can see. This may take some perseverance. Security have been known to move people on from this area.

Airside Spotting

Spotting is quite easy once airside at Stansted. All three piers offer views over the action, however the Ryanair pier is the best with large open areas and windows at the end. The cargo terminal is not visible, however.

Resident Airframes

G-IOIT L1011 Tristar ex Classic Airways.

Nearby Attractions

Imperial War Museum Duxford

Cambridgeshire CB22 4QR ✉ +44 (0) 12 23 83 72 67 ✉ duxford.iwm.org.uk

Possibly Europe's finest aviation museum. IWM Duxford is a former air base which served in both World Wars. Its collections cover the earliest times of flight, through the history of military and commercial aircraft. Of particular note to the enthusiast may be the preserved Concorde, Vickers VC-10 and Viscount, Hawker Siddeley Trident, Bristol Britannia and De Havilland Comet. Open daily (except 24-26 December) from 10am to 6pm (4pm from late October to mid March). Adults £16, Concessions £12.80, Children (0-15) free.

Airlines

Aegean Airlines
airberlin
Air Contractors
Air Europa
Air Malta
Air Moldova
Air Southwest
American Airlines
Asiana Airlines Cargo
Atlantic Airways
Aurigny Air Services
Albanian Airlines
BAC Express Airlines
BH Air
Blue1
Blue Air
Centralwings

Cyprus Airways
Darwin Airline
easyJet
Eastern Airways
El Al
European Air Charter
FedEx Express
First Choice Airways
Germanwings
Global Supply Systems
Iberworld
Iceland Express
Israir
Jet2
KTHY
Martinair Cargo
Monarch Airlines

Norwegian Air Shuttle
Nouvelair
Onur Air
Pegasus Airlines
Royal Jordanian Cargo
Ryanair
Skyways
Spanair
TACV Cabo Verde Airlines
Thomas Cook Airlines
ThomsonFly
Titan Airways
Transavia
Turkish Airlines
UPS
Wizz Air
XL Airways

Hotels

Radisson SAS Stansted Airport

Waltham Close, Stansted Airport, Essex CM24 1PP
+44 (0) 12 79 66 10 12 ⊠ www.stansted.radissonsas.com

A very smart, modern hotel at Stansted with prices at the higher end. Some higher rooms facing the airport have views over the Ryanair pier and Runway 23 threshold. The hotel is only a few metres from the Terminal.

Hilton London Stansted

Round Coppice Road, London Stansted, Essex CM24 1SF
+44 (0) 12 79 68 08 00 ⊠ www.hilton.com

At the opposite end of the airport, close to the M11 and Long Stay Car Parks. The Hilton is another pricey hotel at Stansted. Some rooms facing the airport have views of aircraft on short final to Runway 05, and on the taxiway linking it.

Days Inn

Welcome Break Service Area, J8, M11, Birchanger Green, Bishops Stortford CM23 5QZ
+44 (0) 12 79 65 64 77 ⊠ www.daysinn.com

A much more affordable option is the Days Inn located off the M11 at the entrance to Stansted Airport in the service station. No views of movements are available here, but the hotel is a very short distance from the airport.

Madrid (Barajas)
Spain

MAD | LEMD

Tel: +34 902 40 47 04

Web: www.aena.es

Passengers: 52.1 million (2007)

Overview

Madrid Barajas is on the up. Always Spain's busiest airport, its recent expansion and increased opening to low-cost carriers saw a 13.8% rise in passengers from 2006 to 2007.

Madrid has always held a strong position as a hub airport for national carrier Iberia, and also as the European connection point with Latin America. It is the recent opening of bases here by both easyJet and Ryanair, and new Spanish low-cost carriers Clickair and Vueling that has improved access to the airport, especially to the city break and domestic market.

Enthusiasts have travelled to Madrid for the quality of movements for many years, with a number of spotting locations giving handy access. Although the influx of low-cost carriers may not interest many, they provide cheap access to spotters for quick breaks. The quality of the movements from South America often warrant a trip alone, with many of these airlines not seen elsewhere in Europe.

Naturally Iberia and its feeder airlines are the dominant force, as well as Air Europa and Spanair. A visit of two days or more will usually see the vast majority of their fleets pass through.

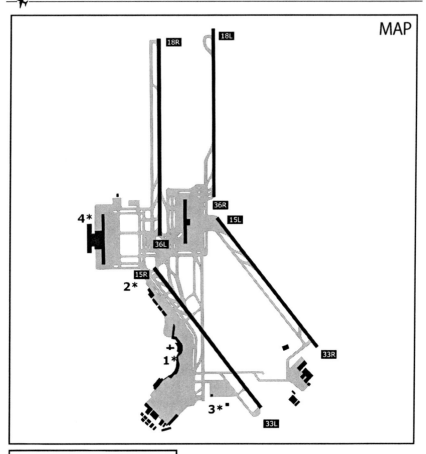

MAP

Frequencies

118.075 Tower RW36L/18R
118.150 Tower RW33L/15R
118.500 Tower Arrivals
118.675 Tower RW36R/18L
118.975 Tower RW33R/15L
120.150 Tower
124.025 Approach
127.500 Approach
121.625 Ground South
121.700 Ground South
121.850 Ground North
123.000 Ground South
123.150 Ground North
123.250 Ground North
130.035 ClearanceDeliveryWest
130.075 Clearance Delivery
130.850 ATIS Departures

Runways

15R/33L 13,451x197ft / 4,100x60m
15L/33R 11,483x197ft / 3,500x60m
18R/36L 14,272x197ft / 4,350x60m
18L/36R 11,483x197ft / 3,500x60m

Spotting Locations

1. Terminal 2 Cafe

This café area in Terminal 2 was the most popular place to spot aircraft at Madrid for many years. It has large windows (slightly tinted, but suitable for photography) and most traffic passing or parking close by. Recently it underwent renovation, and is not a pricier restaurant. The windows are still there, but staying all day is not less welcome. It is reached on the first floor in Terminal 2. There are windows in the hole corridor next to the restaurant.

2. Metro Station Mound

Take the Metro to Barajas, the small town adjacent to the airport. Once there, walk over the white bridge past the restaurant on the left. This raised area will allow you to log almost every movement, even aircraft using the distant new runway and Terminal 4. Excellent photography is possible of aircraft operating nearer to you. It is possible to drive here if you follow signs for Barajas and then head towards the road tunnel under the airport. The mound is alongside. Various places to park exist nearby.

3. Cargo Terminals

Follow the Cargo Terminals road from the passenger terminals (do not join the motor-way). This will take you past the remote ramps. Turn left at the roundabout and follow the road past the catering buildings until you reach the cargo ramp. There are places to park by the side of the road. Photography is possible here of aircraft using Runway 33L. Following the road will take you past the runway threshold, where morning shots are better, and also past the storage area.

4. Car Park P2

This car park is not the ideal spotting location, but it can yield a few of the aircraft parked on the stands around the new terminal's remote pier. Most other movements are better seen elsewhere.

Airside Spotting

Terminal 1 has very limited views once airside. The other Terminals 2 and 3 have some good windows in the departure lounges that will reveal anything parked close by. Terminal 4 is bright and airy with plenty of large windows once airside.

Resident Airframes

EC-ASJ Beech 18 Spantax	EC-EQP Falcon 20
EC-BQZ DC-9-32 preserved	EC-EMX DC-8-62F ex-Cygnus Air
EC-CFE 727-256 ex-Iberia	EC-EVJ Gulfstream I Stellair
EC-CID 727-256 ex-Iberia	EC-EXQ Gulfstream I Drenair
EC-DIA 747-256B ex-Iberia	EC-EXS Gulfstream I Drenair
EC-DIB 747-256B ex-Iberia	EC-GYL F-27-500 Boreal Aviation
EC-DNP 747-256B ex-Iberia	EC-IMY 727-225 ex-Swiftair
EC-HVD 747-256B ex-Iberia	N19BX Gulstream I 19th Hole Corporation
EC-IAF 747-256B ex-Iberia	TU-TDM Gulfstream I 19th Hole Corporation
EC-EXM MD-87 ex-Iberia	N19TZ Gulfstream I 19th Hole Corporation
EC-FLK MD-88 ex-Iberia	TY-24A 727-256 Benin Air Force
EC-EKK Falcon 20	E.15-20/41-6 T-33A Spanish Air Force preserved

Airlines

Aer Lingus	Avianca	Korean Air	Smart Wings
Aeroflot	Blue Air	Lagun Air	Sol Airlines
Aerolineas Argentinas	bmibaby	LAN Airlines	Spanair
Aerolineas de Baleares	British Airways	LAN Ecuador	Swiftair
Aeroméxico	Brussels Airlines	LAN Peru	Swiss International Air Lines
Aerosur	Bulgaria Air	LOT Polish Airlines	Syrian Arab Airlines
airBaltic	Continental Airlines	Lufthansa	TACV Cabo Verde Airlines
airberlin	CSA Czech Airlines	Lviv Airlines	TAER Andalus
Air Algérie	Cubana	Malév Hungarian Airlines	TAM
Air Canada	Cygnus Air	Meridiana	TAP Portugal
Air China	Delta Air Lines	MyAir	TAROM
Air Comet	easyJet	Norwegian Air Shuttle	Thai Airways International
Air Europa	Egyptair	Olympic Airlines	Transavia
Air France	El Al	Pluna	Tunisair
Air Malta	FedEx Express	Portugalia	Turkish Airlines
Air Mauritius	Finnair	Pyrenair	Ukraine International Airlines
Air Moldova	Germanwings	Royal Air Maroc	US Airways
Air Nostrum	Iberia	Royal Jordanian	Varig
Air Pullmantur	Icelandair	Qatar Airways	Vueling
Air Transat	Iberworld	Ryanair	Windjet
Alitalia	Iran Air	Santa Barbara Airlines	
American Airlines	Jet2	SAS	
Atlas Blue	KLM	Saudi Arabian Airlines	

Hotels

Hotel Auditorium Madrid Airport

Avenida de Aragón 400, Madrid 28022 ☒ +34 91 400 44 00 ☒ www.auditoriumhoteles.com

One of the few hotels at Madrid Barajas to offer views of movements. It is situated between runways 01 and 33, and alongside the cargo apron. Higher rooms overlooking the airport offer the best chances, especially with a pole or SBS unit. Can be expensive.

Hotel Tryp Diana

Galeón 27, Madrid 28042 ☒ +34 917 47 13 55 ☒ www.solmelia.com

Situated close to the terminals, and can be very affordable. Some rooms offer views over the cargo apron, though photography is not possible. Offers a free shuttle bus to the airport.

Express by Holiday Inn Madrid Airport

Avenida de Aragón 402, Madrid 28022 ☒ +34 917 48 16 57 ☒ www.hiexpress.com

A little further on from the Hotel Auditorium. Has offers on rooms, which are generally affordable anyway. Some limited views of movements and cargo apron from higher rooms.

Manchester (Ringway)
United Kingdom

MAN | EGCC

Tel: +44 (0) 87 12 71 07 11

Web: www.manchesterairport.co.uk

Passengers: 24 million (2006)

Overview

Manchester has become one of the favourite airports in the UK for enthusiasts thanks to its excellent viewing facilities and fairly varied mix of movements, which can be pleasingly busy at certain times of the day.

Manchester is one of the UK's most important airports and has long been popular with both a charter and scheduled carriers. The north of England gateway has long retained its position as the third busiest in the country, after the Heathrow and Gatwick in the London area. In recent years, coupled with periods of significan expansion, a number of new airlines have started services here. The airport is particularly busy in the summer months.

Manchester Airport has three passenger terminals and a cargo terminal, along with an extensive maintenance area comprising large hangars and bays. The airport has two parallel runways.

Today there is less emphasis on charter services at Manchester - the majority of which now stick to the summer months, which still also see charter carriers from around Europe visiting. Today, as is the case with much of Europe, a larger proportion of flights are of the low-cost variety. Indeed, many of the traditional charter carriers are now turning to low-cost scheduled flights to compete.

Whilst long haul flights were slow to establish at Manchester, today the airport enjoys a number of links across the Atlantic with American Airlines, British Airways, Continental, Delta, PIA and US Airways all plying their trade on a daily basis. In the opposite direction, Emirates, Qatar Airways and Singapore Airlines provide popular links with Asia and the Middle East. A number of cargo carriers provide daily widebody aircraft for added spice.

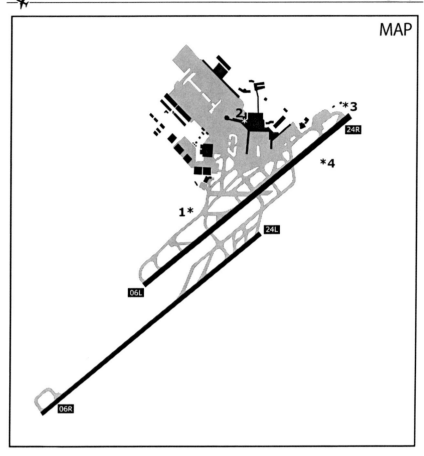

MAP

Frequencies

118.625	Tower
119.400	Tower
118.575	Approach North
135.000	Approach South
121.850	Ground
125.375	Ground
121.700	Clearance Delivery
121.350	Director
121.975	ATIS Departures
128.175	ATIS

Runways

06R/24L 9,997x150ft / 3,047x46m
06L/24R 10,000x150ft / 3,048x46m

Resident Airframes

G-BOAC
Concorde British Airways preserved

G-IRJX RJX 100 preserved

G-DMCA DC-10-30
ex-Monarch preserved nose section

G-AWZK Trident 3B BEA preserved

G-AVFG Trident 2E fire service

SET 72 Jetstream 61
unfinished airframe, fire service

Spotting Locations

1. Aviation Viewing Park

What must be the best official viewing facility in the UK is located at Manchester. The Aviation Viewing Park (AVP) was built on the north side of Runway 06L/24R to replace facilities lost when the new runway was built and terminals extended. Purpose-built mounds raise the enthusiast over the height of the fence to allow photography of aircraft on the runway and taxiway. Also at the AVP is a hobby shop, café, toilets and various preserved airliners – some of which are open to the public. These include a DC-10 section, Concorde, Trident and Avro RJX. It currently costs £4 per car, or £1 per pedestrian. The AVP is open daily (except Christmas Day) from 8.30am till dusk.

2. Multi-Storey Car Park

For many years the top level of the Short Stay Car Park outside Terminal 1 was also the spotter's choice. It offered fantastic views over the cargo and maintenance ramps, as well as Terminal 2, parts of Terminal 1, and the runways in the distance. Cafe and hobby shop facilities were also located here. However, as of late 2006 the area has been cleared and the shop relocated to the arrivals hall of Terminal 1. Spotting and photography are still possible from the car park, albeit unofficially. This is a good spot to log what's not visible from the Aviation Viewing Park.

3. Airport Hotel Pub

Located at the threshold of Runway 24R. The beer garden here backs up to the taxiway and holding point for the runway and is ideal for landing shots. A very pleasant summer afternoon can be held here, with food and refreshments on tap.

4. South Side

Along the southern boundary of the airport, a number of unofficial spots can be reached by car which offer great opportunities to take photographs of aircraft on the runways, and views across most of the terminal areas. From the Airport Hotel, take a right and the third exit at the roundabout. At the lights, turn right again onto Moss Lane. Half a mile further on, you will find an area suitable for parking (being careful not to obstruct the gate) with the airport in front of you.

Airside Spotting

Spotting is possible once airside in all three terminals thanks to large windows in all gate areas. Terminal 2 is a little far off to see movements at the other terminals and on the runways. You will see all movements from Terminals 1 and 3 if you are there long enough.

Security

Manchester Airport thankfully understands aviation enthusiasts and has always tried its best to provide for the hobby and visitors. Despite the unpopular decisions to close the old rooftop terraces, most spotters understand this was necessary in the face of expansion and security, and are more than happy with the facilities provided at the Aviation Viewing Park.

Recently the Greater Manchester Police have issued a poster around the popular spotting locations at the airport urging enthusiasts to play their part in the fight against terrorism by reporting any suspicious activity to them.

Airlines

Adria Airways	British Airways	First Choice Airways	Ryanair
Aer Arann	Brussels Airlines	FlyGlobespan	SAS
Aer Lingus	Bulgaria Air	Flybe.	Saudi Arabian Airlines
Aeroflot-Cargo	Cathay Pacific Cargo	Flyjet	Singapore Airlines
arberlin	Centralwings	Futura	SkyEurope
AirBlue	China Airlines Cargo	Great Wall Airlines	SwissInternationalAirLines
Air China Cargo	City Airline	Icelandair	Syrianair
Air Contractors	Continental Airlines	Jett8 Airlines Cargo	Thomas Cook Airlines
Air Europa	CSA Czech Airlines	Jet2	ThomsonFly
Air France	Cyprus Airways	KLM	Titan Airways
Air Malta	Delta Air Lines	KTHY	TUIfly.com
Air Southwest	Eastern Airways	Libyan Arab Airways	Turkish Airlines
American Airlines	easyJet	Lufthansa	US Airways
Astraeus	Emirates	MNG Cargo Airlines	Virgin Atlantic
Aurigny Air Services	Eithad Airways	Monarch Airlines	VLM Airlines
Austrian Airlines	Eurocypria Airlines	Olympic Airways	Volareweb
Belavia	Euromanx	Onur Air	XL Airways
BH Air	FedEx Express	PIAPakistanInt.Airlines	Zoom Airlines
bmi, bmibaby	Finnair	Qatar Airways	Zoom Airlines UK

Hotels

Radisson SAS Hotel

Chicago Avenue, Manchester M90 3RA ☒ +44 (0) 161 490 5000 ☒ www.radissonsas.com
The best hotel for spotting at Manchester. Located behind Terminal 2, rooms on high
floors overlook the aprons and the runways in the distance. The restaurant also offers
this view. Some good opportunities for photographs with a long lens. Rarely cheap.

Hilton Manchester Airport

Outwood Lane, Manchester M90 4WP ☒ +44 (0) 16 14 35 30 40 ☒ www.hilton.com
Located close to the terminals, though with very few views of aircraft movements.
Rooms can be reasonably priced. The terminals are a very short walk from this hotel.

Nearby Attractions

Woodford Aerodrome

Woodford is an airfield located to the south of Manchester which is operated by BAE
Systems. Many Avro and BAe aircraft were built here. Today the Nimrod MRA4 is being
produced. A number of derelict and preserved aircraft, particularly BAe ATPs, can be
found here. Views possible from golf course on the airfield's south eastern edge.

Manchester Museum of Science and Industry

Located in the heart of Manchester, this museum has a whole building dedicated to
aircraft. Collection includes a Dragon Rapide, Avro 504, Bristol Belvedere, Bristol
Sycamore, Trident 3B cockpit and many more. Museum is open daily 10am-5pm except
24-26 December and 1 January. Free entry.

Milan (Linate)
Italy

LIN | LIML

Tel: +39 (0) 274 85 22 00
Web: www.sea-aeroportimilano.it
Passengers: 9.6 million (2006)

Overview

The original, yet much smaller airport of Milan is Linate. It is situated much closer to the city than the larger Malpensa, however it has always been limited by space and facilities. When Malpensa opened its new terminal in 2000, much of Linate's traffic moved there.

Despite this, the airport is still popular with a number of international carriers from around Europe, some low-cost airlines, and a few cargo operators. It is also a haven of domestic airliners which are rarely seen outside of Italy, and often don't venture to Malpensa. Because of it's closer proximity to the centre of Milan, Linate is also popular with business users and their private aircraft.

The terminal building is fairly antiquated now, but suitable for its purpose. On the opposite side of the runway is a ramp for executive and government aircraft, as well as a smaller general aviation runway.

Linate has some good opportunities for spotting, as long as precautions are taken not to rouse the suspicions of the local police or security personnel, especially with the government transport movements.

MAP

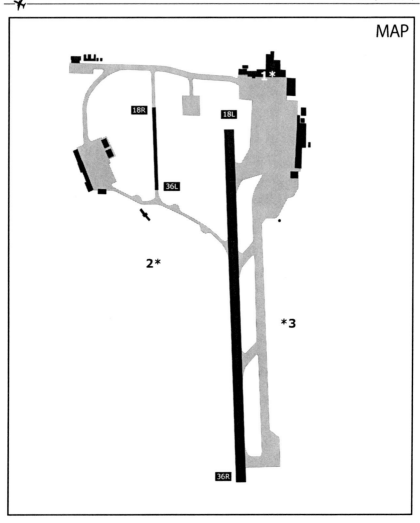

Frequencies

118.100 Tower
119.250 Tower
125.275 Approach
132.700 Approach
126.300 DeparturesEast/South
126.750 DeparturesEast/North
119.250 Ground
121.800 Ground
116.000 ATIS

Runways

18R/36L 1,972x72ft / 601x22m
18L/36R 8,005x197ft / 2,440x60m

Spotting Locations

1. Terminal

Inside the terminal, the only real opportunity to spot is from the upstairs café which overlooks the apron and stands. Food is not cheap here, but it's advisable to purchase some to justify your stay. The café can be reached by following signs.

2. Perimeter Road

From the terminal, head in the direction of Milan. Shortly after passing the northern boundary, take an immediate left on to Viale dell'Aviazione. This road will lead past the military side of the airport, and eventually past a number of spots where views across the airfield can be had. Most aircraft can be read off from here with a good pair of binoculars. Following on along the road, and through the small village of Linate, the road loops around the end of Runway 36R. Various opportunities for photography can be had around this area.

3. Cemetery

One of the most popular spots around the perimeter is the cemetery. After passing the end of Runway 36R, turn left on to Via Walter Tobagi and pass through the industrial estate. Eventually, turn left at the T-junction on to Via 4 Novembre and follow to the end. The car park next to the cemetery fronts the perimeter fence. Aircraft using the runway and taxiway are at extremely close quarters here. The terminal can not be seen, however.

Airside Spotting

Inside the terminal's departure lounges, most movements can be read off through the windows.

Nearby Attractions

Malpensa Airport

Malpensa is the largest and busiest of Milan's airports, although recently Alitalia have announced changes that will see most of their operation move to Rome. Low-cost carriers are set to increase their presence. Otherwise, airlines from around Europe, North America, and Asia fly in every day.

Bergamo Orio al Serio Airport

Milan's original low-cost airport, taken on board by Ryanair and now a lively airport in its own right. Most of Europe's low-cost airlines show up here, as well as some charter carriers. Military and stored aircraft are also in residence.

Airlines

Aer Lingus

Air France

Air One

Alitalia

Austrian Airlines

British Airways

easyJet

Eurofly

Iberia

ItAli Airlines

KLM

Lufthansa

Meridiana

Olympic Airlines

SAS

TAP Portugal

Volare Airlines

Windjet

Hotels

Holiday Inn Milan Linate Airport

Via Buozzi 2, Peschiera Borromeo 20078 ⊠ +39 (0) 255 36 01 ⊠ www.hotelcervo.it

This is a standard Holiday Inn hotel, with good facilities and clean rooms. It is one of the more affordable options for Linate, however due to its distance there are no views of aircraft movements.

Air Hotel

Via F. Baracca 2, Novegro di Segrate 20090 ⊠ +39 (0) 270200009 ⊠ www.airhotel.com

This is the closest hotel to the airport, and most convenient for travellers and visitors. The hotel is smart, but can be expensive most of the year. No views of aircraft movements.

Milan (Malpensa)
Italy

MXP | LIMC

Tel: +39 (0) 274 85 22 00
Web: www.sea-aeroportimilano.it
Passengers: 21.7 million (2006)

Overview

The modern Malpensa airport has been a fine airport since its revamp opened in 2000, putting the crowded old facilities behind (albeit as the secondary charter/low-cost terminal). The modern new Terminal 1 is spread over three areas, with new additions recently made. At the southern end is a cargo terminal, whilst to the north are maintenance facilities.

The older Terminal 2 is situated between the long parallel runways, and is rarely busy.

Recent news which threatens to ruin the appeal of the airport is the announcement by Alitalia, who base a large number of aircraft here, that it is moving the aircraft to Rome. This will vastly reduce the number of flights by the national airline at this airport.

The immediate reaction was by easyJet and Ryanair, who plan to add a large presence at Malpensa. easyJet already operate a number of flights from here and Linate, whilst Ryanair operate from nearby Bergamo airport.

As with all Italian airports, the police and security presence is obvious, and spotters do not always have their approval. However, a number of spots around the airport are frequented by spotters, and give the chance to log all aircraft and photograph many.

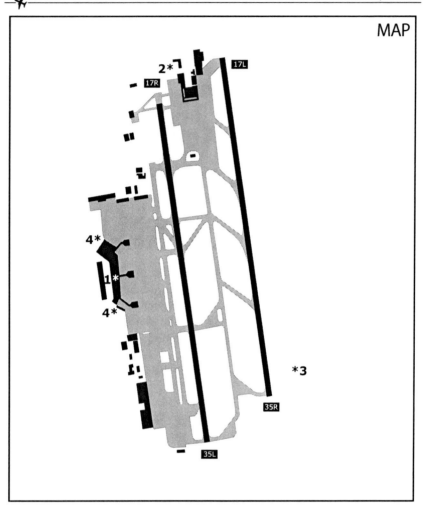

MAP

Frequencies

119.000 Tower RW17L/35R
128.350 Tower RW17R/35L
125.275 Approach
132.700 Approach
126.300 Departures South
126.750 Departures North
120.900 Clearance Delivery
121.825 Ground North
121.900 Ground West
120.025 ATIS
121.625 ATIS Departures

Runways

17R/35L 12,861x197ft / 3,920x60m
17L/35R 12,861x197ft / 3,920x60m

Spotting Locations

1. Terminal 1
At the departures level in Terminal 1, large windows front the gates, aprons and distant runways. Simply walk past the rows of check-in counters. For a little more discretion, head to the right and find a hidden alcove behind the Benetton shop and play area. This offers the same view, with limited views over the cargo ramp, but is rarely patrolled by security. All movements can be seen from here, however those at Terminal 2 are harder to read off. Photography is not easy through the tinted glass.

2. Terminal 2
The short-stay car park outside Terminal 2 is suitable for reading off aircraft parked on one side of the terminal's apron, and also to read off aircraft using Runways 17L/R.

3. Far Side
From Terminal 1, a road named Via Strada Provincia runs south alongside the SS336 motorway, turning into Via del Gregge. Follow this to a small roundabout, and take the left exit, crossing the motorway onto Via Molinelli. Follow this road past the ends of Runways 35L/R, then turn left onto Via Case Sparse. Eventually you will reach a small car park and play area on the left. Spotters regularly congregate here. This spot is great for photographs, especially if you use the picnic benches or climbing frame! Movements on both runways can easily be read off.

4. Around Terminal 1
Walking around 500 metres in either direction from the entrance to Terminal 1 will bring you to spots where aircraft can be seen using the taxiways and nearest runway. Photography is only possible with a step or small ladder. Recent work around the Alitalia Crew Briefing Centre to the north has drastically restricted views, however.

Airside Spotting
In Terminal 1, the satellites have excellent views over the action on both runways. Most movements can be read from here. Terminal 2 is a little more frustrating, with very limited views once airside.

Nearby Attractions

Linate Airport
The original Milan airport, situated much closer to the city centre, still handles a decent amount of traffic. It is a good place to catch the domestic aircraft of Alitalia and Air One which are rarely seen outside of Italy. See separate entry.

Bergamo Orio al Serio Airport
Milan's original low-cost airport, taken on board by Ryanair and now a lively airport in its own right. Most of Europe's low-cost airlines show up here, as well as some charter carriers. Military and stored aircraft are also in residence.

Airlines

Aegean Airlines	Blue Panorama	Israir	Qatar Airways
Aer Lingus	British Airways	ItAli Airlines	Rossiya
Aerocondor	Brussels Airlines	Japan Airlines	Royal Air Maroc
Aeroflot	Cargoitalia	Jet4you	Royal Jordanian
airBaltic	Cargolux	Jet Airways	SAS
Air Atlanta Icelandic	Cathay Pacific Cargo	Karthago	Saudi Arabian Airlines
Air China	China Airlines Cargo	KD-Avia	Singapore Airlines
Air Dolomiti	Clickair	KLM	Spanair
Air Europa	Continental Airlines	Korean Air Cargo	Sterling
Air France	CSA Czech Airlines	Libyan Airlines	Sun D'Or
Air Italy	Cyprus Airways	Livingston Energy Flight	SunExpress
Air Madagascar	Delta Air Lines	LOT Polish Airlines	SwissInternationalAirLines
Air Malta	DHL Airways	LTEInternationalAirways	Syrian Arab Airlines
Air Mauritius	easyJet	Lufthansa	TACV Cabo Verde Airlines
Aor Moldova	Egyptair	Lufthansa Cargo	TAM
Air One	El Al	Luxair	TAP Portugal
Air Seychelles	Emirates	MalévHungarianAirlines	TAROM
African Safari Airways	Emirates Cargo	MASkargo	Thai Airways International
Alitalia	Estonian Air	MEA Middle East Airlines	Tradewinds
Alitalia Cargo	Etihad Airways	Meridiana	Tunisair
AMC Airlines	Eurofly	Mistral Air	Turkish Airlines
American Airlines	FedEx Express	MNG Airlines	Ukraine International
Arkia	Finnair	Neos	US Airways
Atlas Air	Flybe.	Niki	Uzbekistan Airways
Atlas Blue	FlyLal	Nippon Cargo Airlines	Varig
Austrian Airlines	Futura	Nouvelair	Volare Airlines
Azerbaijan Airlines	Germanwings	Olympic Airlines	Volareweb
Belle Air	Iberia	PIA Pakistan Int. Airlines	Vueling
Blue1	Icelandair	Polar Air Cargo	West Air Sweden
Blue Line	Iran Air	Polet Airlines	World Airways

Hotels

Hotel Cervo

Via de Pinedo 1, Somma Lombardo 21019 ☎ +39 (0) 331 230821 ✉ www.hotelcervo.it

An affordable hotel only minutes from Terminal 1. Offers shuttle service from the airport. No rooms have views of aircraft movements, but this is regarded as the most convenient hotel for spotters.

Crowne Plaza

Via Ferrarin 7 Case Nuove, Somma Lombardo 21019
+39 (0) 33 12 11 61 ✉ www.crowneplaza.com

Located between both terminals, with transfers available to either. Pricier option for staying at the airport, but convenient nevertheless. Views of aircraft movements are not possible.

Munich (Franz Josef Strauss)
Germany

MUC | EDDM

Tel: +49 (0) 89 97 500
Web: www.munich-airport.de
Passengers: 30.8 million (2006)

Overview

Munich has in recent years become Germany's second busiest airport, and a much more important hub for Lufthansa than had been the case previously, since its Frankfurt base has become increasingly busy.

It was built to replace the old Riem airport, and opened in 1992. You will find it is a very modern airport with top-class facilities – it was even voted "Best Airport in Europe" in 2007.

Terminal 2 was opened in 2003 to cope with the increase in traffic here, and a third runway is currently being planned. Much of the increase in traffic is due to the saturation of Frankfurt.

Like Frankfurt, Munich is another place to see a large number of Russian-built airliners from eastern Europe and the former Soviet states. There are also a large number of Turkish airlines serving the airport.

As with most German airports, facilities provided for watching aircraft are of excellent quality and very popular with spotters and locals alike. The small collection of preserved historic airliners adds interest to the viewing facilities.

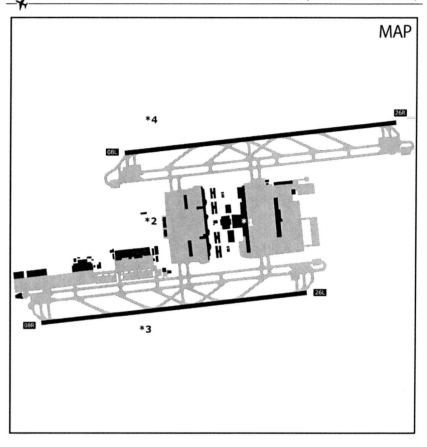

MAP

Frequencies

118.700 Tower North
120.500 Tower South
120.775 ApproachSouthRW08R/26L
123.900 ApproachNorthRW08L/26R
127.950 ApproachSouthRW08R/26L
128.025 ApproachNorthRW08L/26R
128.250 Radar
121.725 Clearance
118.825 Director
121.700 Ramp East
121.775 Ramp West
121.925 Ramp West
121.825 Ground South
121.975 Ground North
123.125 ATIS

Runways

08R/26L   13,123x197ft / 4,000x60m
08L/26R 13,123x197ft / 4,000x60m

Spotting Locations

1. Terminal 2 Terrace

Atop Terminal 2 is a good place to log aircraft, and photography is also possible, although glass surrounds the deck. Sadly many movements at Terminal 1 are not visible from here, although aircraft can often be seen on the runway. Terminal 2 is used by Lufthansa and its Star Alliance partners. Good binoculars are required to read off aircraft on the business ramp to the left. This is the most popular choice, although many prefer to take a log of Terminal 1 aircraft from the Mound before moving here.

2. Viewing Hill (The Mound)

The second official viewing location is the Mound, located between the runways close to the central terminal area. As the name suggests, this is an elevated position with views over the ramps and runways over two levels. It is open daily and has a €1 charge. Also at the spot is an aviation shop and a few preserved historic aircraft, including a DC-3, Junkers Ju-52, and Lockheed Constellation. It is possible to walk to the Mound, however the S-Bahn train service stops here one stop before the terminal.

3. Runway 8R/26L

A road runs the length of this runway, with various places to stop and get close-up shots of the action. Be careful not to obstruct emergency gates.

4. Runway 8L/26R

A road runs the length of this runway, with various places to stop and get close-up shots of the action. Be careful not to obstruct emergency gates.

Airport Tours

Tours by coach are available from the Visitors Centre Car Park, which give airside trips around the ramps of both terminals, passing the runways and fire station and other buildings. Lasts 50 minutes and gives good close-up opportunities for photographs. Bookings should be made in advance through the airport website.

Airside Spotting

Once airside in both terminals, there are windows around the departure areas which offer limited views of the stands.

Resident Airframes

D-ANOY Ju-52 Lufthansa preserved
D-ALEM Constellation Lufthansa preserved
HB-IRN DC-3 Swissair preserved

Airlines

Adria Airways	Cirrus Airlines	InterSky	S7 Airlines
Aegean Airlines	Clickair	Israir	SAS
Aer Lingus	Condor	Jat Airways	Saudi Arabian Airlines
Aeroflot	Croatia Airlines	KD-Avia	South African Airways
African Safari Airways	CSA Czech Airlines	KLM	Spanair
airBaltic	Delta Air Lines	Korean Air	Sun D'Or
airberlin	DHL Air	Korean Air Cargo	SwissInternationalAirLines
Air Canada	easyJet	LOT Polish Airlines	TACV Cabo Verde Airlines
Air China	Egyptair	LTU International	TAP Portugal
Air France	El Al	Lufthansa	TAROM
Air Malta	Emirates	Lufthansa Cargo	ThaiAirwaysInternational
Air Mauritius	Emirates Cargo	Luxair	TNT Airways
Alitalia	Estonian Air	MalévHungarianAirlines	Transaero Airlines
Arkia	Etihad Airways	Niki	Tunisair
Austrian Airlines	Eurocypria Airlines	Norwegian Air Shuttle	Turkish Airlines
Bluebird Cargo	FedEx Express	OLT	United Airlines
Blue Wings	Finnair	Olympic Airlines	Ural Airlines
British Airways	FlyLal	Pegasus Airlines	US Airways
Brussels Airlines	Germanwings	Polet Airlines	UTair Aviation
Cargoitalia	GlobalSupplySystems	Qatar Airways	West Air Sweden
Carpatair	HamburgInternational	Qatar Airways Cargo	
Cathay Pacific Cargo	Iberia	Rossiya	
Cimber Air	Icelandair	Royal Jordanian	

Hotels

NH Munich Airport Hotel

Lohstrasse 21, 85445 Schwaig/Oberding, Munich ☏ +4981229670 ⌨ www.nh-hotels.com
Affordable hotel, located 4km from the airport. Shuttles to the terminals every 30 minutes cost €5. There are no acceptable views of aircraft from this hotel.

Hotel Kempinski

Terminalstrasse Mitte 20, 85356 Munich ☏ +498997820 ⌨ www.kempinski-airport.de
A modern hotels in the centre of the terminal area at Munich Airport, with 389 room and suites. Slightly pricier, with rooms starting at €208, but perfect for convenience. Rooms on the upper floors have limited views of the terminal aprons.

Mövenpick Hotel Munich Airport

Ludwigstrasse 43, 85399 Munich ☏ +49 81 18 880 ⌨ www.moevenpick-hotels.com
Located close to the end of Runway 8R. Some rooms have limited views of aircraft on final approach. The viewing locations are a short walk/drive from here.

Palma de Mallorca (Son Sant Joan)
Spain

PMI | LEPA
Tel: +34 902 40 47 04
Web: www.aena.es
Passengers: 23.2 million (2007)

Overview

Palma has cemented itself at the heart of one of the most popular holiday destinations in Europe, on the Balearic island of Mallorca. Millions flock here year round from all over Northern Europe. Its airport is currently the third largest in Spain, and is one of the busiest in Europe during peak summer months.

All manner of charter and leisure airlines have frequented Palma since the 1970s, with the advent of the package holiday. Today this is still the case, however the low-cost airlines have muscled their way in offering cheaper flight-only deals at the cost of many charter airlines. airberlin in particular have become one of the largest users of the airport. In addition to this, Spanish national and domestic carriers also make up a significant proportion of movements – both inter-island and to various points on the mainland.

The variety of visitors, particularly in the summer, and good weather makes Palma popular amongst spotters. Various locations around the perimeter allow good photographs, and a number of nearby hotels have views of the movements. During the summer months weekends can prove very fruitful.

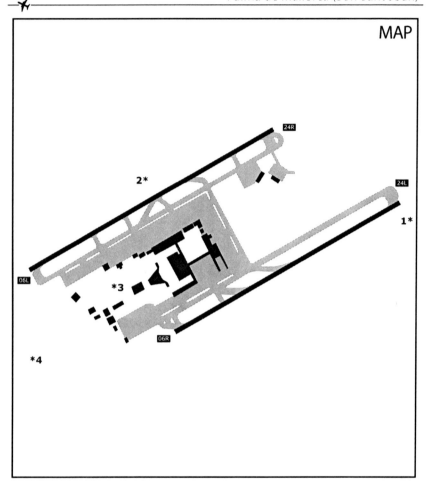

MAP

Frequencies

118.300 Tower
118.450 Tower
118.950 Approach
119.150 Approach
119.400 Approach
121.600 Clearance Delivery
121.700 Ground South
121.900 Ground North
119.250 ATIS

Runways

06L/24R 10,728x148ft / 3,270x45m
06R/24L 9,842x148ft / 3,000x45m

Spotting Locations

1. Runway 24L Mound

Ideal for morning to mid-afternoon photography. This mound is situated alongside the threshold of the runway on the road to Manicor, off the motorway leading to the terminal.

2. Perimeter Road

The road running alongside runway 06L/24R is good for afternoon photography and logging. This is also off the road from Palma to Manicor, turning right before the first service station and down the track on the left as the road enters a hairpin. There are plenty of parking spots and benches along the track.

3. Perimeter

If photography is not an immediate concern, it is possible to walk around the airport complex and perimeter to log all aircraft parked on the various ramps. The car rental car parks are a good place to start. A push bike is useful for getting around as the area covered is large.

4. Beach

When arrivals are coming from the sea, as they often do, the nearby beach is fine for logging and some photography.

Airside Spotting

The terminal at Palma is spread out over a large area, and spotting can be frustrating once airside as the windows are limited and movements often go unseen from any particular point.

Resident Airframes

EC-BZO Convair 990 ex-Spantax

Nearby Attractions

Son Bonnet

The other airfield on Mallorca is Son Bonnet, situated a few miles northwest of Palma city. It is a general aviation airfield with a number of resident aircraft and the occasional larger movement. A derelict DC-3 can be found here, registered N330. Views can be had from various places around the airfield.

Airlines

Aer Lingus	Jetairfly
airberlin	LagunAir
Air Europa	Lauda Air
Air Nostrum	Lufthansa
Austrian Airlines	Luxair
bmi	Martinair
bmibaby	Monarch Airlines
British Airways	Niki
Brussels Airlines	Norwegian Air Shuttle
Bulgaria Air	Ryanair
Centralwings	SAS
Clickair	Spanair
Condor	Sterling
easyJet	Swiss International Air Lines
Estonian Air	Thomas Cook Airlines
First Choice Airways	Thomas Cook Airlines Belgium
Flybe.	ThomsonFly
FlyGlobespan	Transavia
Germanwings	Travel Service
Hamburg International	TUIfly.com
Iberia	Wizz Air
Jet2	XL Airways

Hotels

Hotel Helios

Carre Pollacra 5, 07610 Palma (Mallorca) ⊠ +34 971 264400 ⊠ www.helios-hotels.com

Airport facing rooms on the 5th floor have excellent views from balconies of the traffic on runways 06L/R, and many of the ground movements and aprons. The hotel is very affordable, even in summer.

Hotel Hoteur Linda

Carre Octavi August 2, 07610 Palma (Mallorca) ⊠ +34 971 26 29 82

A popular hotel which as rooms overlooking arrivals to runway 06L and departures from 06R. Also limited views of aircraft on the ground. Try even numbered rooms in the range 514-526.

Paris (Charles de Gaulle Roissy)

France

CDG | LFPG

Tel: +41 (0) 1 48 62 22 80
Web: www.aeroportsdeparis.fr
Passengers: 59.9 million (2007)

Overview

Charles de Gaulle, or Roissy, is the busiest airport in France and the second busiest in Europe in terms of passenger numbers. In terms of movements and cargo it was Europe's busiest in 2006.

Charles de Gaulle is the main operating base for Air France, and a number of other French airlines. It handles flights from every corner of the globe, and across Europe. Surprisingly for such a busy airport, it also handles a number of low-cost airlines.

The original Terminal 1 is now fairly old and has a curious design. Nevertheless, it still handles most of the non-Air France traffic at the airport. Air France and its partners use Terminal 2, and Terminal T9 is used by the low-cost and charter airlines. Large cargo facilities can be found to the west of both terminal areas, with the airport handling FedEx's main European distribution, and also Air France Cargo's operations. A number of other cargo airlines pass through.

France has made a name for itself in recent years for proving difficult with aviation enthusiasts. Despite a number of good locations, authorities have placed a ban on photography, and can be less than welcoming to spotters. It always helps to have a letter written in French explaining your plans.

To apply for a permit to photography at Paris,
e-mail xavier.huby@seine-saint-denis.pref.gouv.fr.

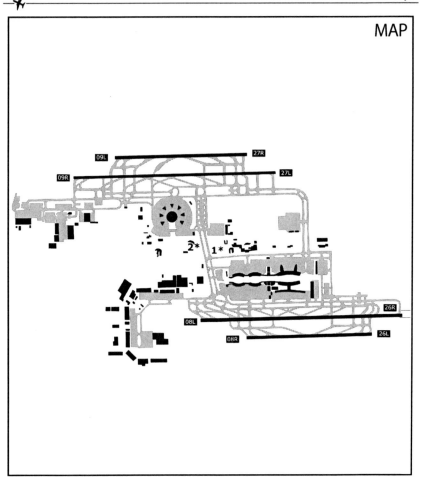

MAP

Frequencies

119.250 Tower Terminal 1
120.650 Tower Terminal 2
125.825 Approach
126.425 Approach
124.350 DepartureTerminal2
133.375 DepartureTerminal2
121.600 Ground Terminal 1
121.800 Ground Terminal 2
126.175 ATIS
127.125 ATIS

Resident Airframes

F-BVFFConcordeAirFrancepreserved

Runways

08R/26L 8,858x197ft / 2,700x60m
08L/26R 13,829x148ft / 4,215x45m
09R/27L 13,780x148ft / 4,200x45m
09L/27R 8,858x197ft / 2,700x60m

Spotting Locations

1. Mound

The classic spot at Charles de Gaulle where most spotters congregate to watch the action. Its raised position makes it fine for photography, and its location means most aircraft movements will at least be visible if not in close range for photographs. The spot is located alongside the Hilton hotel and train station between all three terminals, and easily reached by foot.

2. Motorway Bridge

A little to the west of the first spot, and closer to Terminal 1 is the motorway bridge. From here aircraft can be seen taxiing. It is fine for photography. There are no views of Terminal 2, however.

Airside Spotting

All three passenger terminals have views of aircraft movements which will satisfy those wishing to log. Terminal 2 is by far the best, and its clear glass windows are even good for photography. The piers enable you to see most movements on this side of the airport, and some on the northern runways. Terminal 1 is a little restricted, but you can at least see the aircraft parked around you.

Nearby Attractions

Paris Orly Airport

The second airport of Paris. See separate guide. Can be reached on the RER train directly from Charles de Gaulle.

Le Bourget Airport

Only a 10 minute drive, or 30 minute bus journey (line 350 or 351) from Charles de Gaulle, Le Bourget is an excellent diversion. It handles many of the executive jet traffic landing at Paris, and is also famous for the bi-annual Paris Air Salon. The museum on site has an interesting collection of airliners, including a Boeing 707, 747, Caravelle, Dassault Mercure and Concorde.

Musée de l'air et de l'espace

93352 Le Bourget ✆ +33 (0) 1 49 92 70 62

Open daily except Monday from 10am to 6pm (5pm in winter). The museum is free, but tickets must be bought to enter certain aircraft.

Hotels

Hilton Paris Charles de Gaulle

Roissypôle, Rue de Rome, BP16461 Tremblay En France 95708
+33 (0) 1 49 19 77 77 ✉ www.hilton.com

Situated between the two terminal areas. Rooms on the fourth floor or higher offer views of the taxiways and some aprons – particularly rooms ending in 01 and 29. Windows next to the lifts also give views over the holding points. Slightly pricey.

Ibis Hotel

Roissy Aéroport Cedex, BP 11122 Roissy 95701 ☒ +33 (0)1 49 19 19 21 ☒ www.ibishotel.com

A more affordable option is the large Ibis hotel. North facing rooms have views over Terminal 2 and northern runways, and south facing have views over Terminal 1 and the charter terminal. The hotel is also located next to the Mount spotting location.

Pullman Paris CDG Airport Hotel

Zone Centrale Ouest, BP 20248 Roissy 95713 ☒ +33 (0)1 49 19 29 29 ☒ www.sofitel.com

Formely the Sofitel. Another hotel located between the terminals at Charles de Gaulle. East-facing rooms have views of the taxiways and most movements. Hotel can be pricey, however.

Airlines

Adria Airways	Astraeus	Gabon Airlines	PIA Pakistan International Airlines
Aer Lingus	Atlas Blue	Georgian Airways	Portugalia
Aeroflot	Austrian Airlines	Germanwings	Qatar Airways
Aeroméxico	Azerbaijan Airlines	Gulf Air	Rossiya
Afriqiyah Airways	Belavia	Iberia	Royal Air Maroc
Aigle Azur	Blue1	Iberworld	Royal Jordanian
airBaltic	Blue Line	Icelandair	SAS
Air Algérie	bmibaby	Iceland Express	SATA Internacional
Air Austral	British Airways	InterSky	Saudi Arabian Airlines
Air Cairo	Bulgaria Air	Israir	Singapore Airlines
Air Canada	Cathay Pacific	Japan Airlines	Smart Wings
Air China	China Eastern Airlines	Jat Airways	SriLankan Airlines
Air Comet	China Southern Airlines	Jet2	Sterling
Air Contractors	Clickair	Karthago Airlines	Sun D'Or
Air Europa	Continental Airlines	KD-Avia	Swiss International Air Lines
Air France	Corendon Airlines	Kenya Airways	TAAG Angola Airlines
Air France Cargo	Croatia Airlines	KLM	TACV Cabo Verde Airlines
Air India	CSA Czech Airlines	Korean Air	TAM
Air Madagascar	Cyprus Airways	Kuwait Airways	TAP Portugal
Air Mauritius	Daallo Airlines	LOT Polish Airlines	TAROM
Air Mediterranée	Delta Air Lines	Lufthansa	Thai Airways International
Air Memphis	easyJet	Luxair	Turkmenistan Airlines
Air Moldova	Egyptair	Malaysia Airlines	Ukraine International Airlines
Air Nostrum	El Al	Malév Hungarian Airlines	United Airlines
Air One	Emirates	Mauritania Airways	UPS
Air Seychelles	Ethiopian Airlines	MEA Middle East Airlines	US Airways
Air Tahiti Nui	Etihad Airways	Meridiana	Uzbekistan Airways
Air Transat	EVA Air	MyAir	Varig
Alitalia	Evolavia	Niki	Vietnam Airlines
All Nippon Airways	FedEx Express	Northwest Airlines	Vueling
American Airlines	Finnair	Nouvelair	Windjet
Arkia	Flybe.	Olympic Airlines	XL Airways France
Armavia	FlyLal	Onur Air	Yemenia
Asiana Airlines	Free Bird Airlines	Open Skies	Zoom Airlines

Paris (Orly)
France

ORY | LFPO

Tel: +34 (0) 1 49 75 15 15
Web: www.aeroportsdeparis.fr
Passengers: 26.4 million (2007)

Overview

Orly is the second busiest airport in both Paris and France as a whole. Whilst nearby Charles de Gaulle is larger and busier, Orly is still very much worth a visit as most of Air France's domestic network operates from here, as well as a number of long haul flights. Many other scheduled, charter and low-cost airlines use Orly which also wouldn't be seen at Charles de Gaulle.

Orly has two terminals – West and South. There is an official viewing location in the South Terminal which is adequate for viewing most movements. Many photographers choose to move to various spots around the perimeter for better results, however.

The airport is easily linked to Paris and Charles de Gaulle by the road, bus and train network.

As with Charles de Gaulle, aircraft photography here is officially banned, and it will often help your case if you have a letter with you to present to authorities (see appendix). These will usually gain permission to continue.

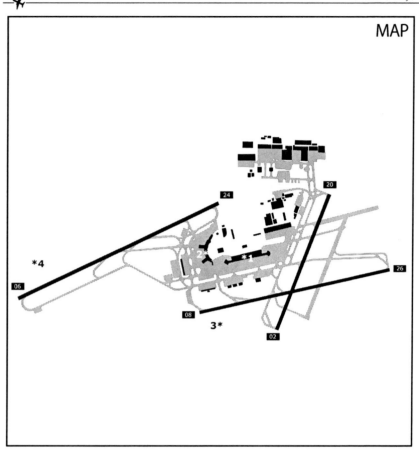

MAP

Frequencies

118.700 Tower
120.500 Tower
118.850 Approach
123.875 Approach/Departures
124.450 Approach
128.375 Approach
127.750 Departures
121.700 Ground
121.825 Ground
126.500 ATIS
131.350 ATIS

Runways

02/20	7,874x197ft / 2,400x60m
06/24	11,975x148ft / 3,650x45m
08/26	10,892x148ft / 3,320x45m

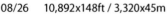

Spotting Locations

1. South Terminal Observation Deck

The South Terminal has an outdoor observation area which can be reached from within the terminal. This is a good location for logging most of the airport's movements, and photography is possible (although mostly south-facing). The deck is free to enter, however it is often closed. If this is the case, windows inside offer a similar view.

2. West Terminal

Upstairs in the West Terminal are a number of windows around the food court which allow views over the aircraft gates.

3. Runway 08

Take the N7 motorway underneath the airport from the South Terminal. At the first crossroads turn right. Then at the large roundabout, take the third exit – Avenue d'Alsace-Lorraine. At the end, there are places to view aircraft lining up on the runway around Rue des Mimosas. Photography is possible.

4. Runway 06

Take the A106 away from the terminals towards Paris. Leave the motorway at Rungis and head along Rue Notre Dame. Turn left at the roundabout on to Rue de la Gare, which turns into the D167a. This eventually runs along the northern perimeter of the runway. There are places to spot and photograph aircraft around the threshold.

Airside Spotting

Both terminals have windows around the gates, and offer similar views as the food courts over the aircraft parked and operating around. The South Terminal is the best overall for airside spotting.

Resident Airframes

SU-DAS A300B4 fire trainer
F-WTSA Concorde preserved
F-ARIT, marked F-BTTJ Dassault Mercure Air Inter preserved
F-BVPZ Caravelle Athis-Paray Aviation
F-GCVI Caravelle Air Inter preserved

Nearby Attractions

Charles de Gaulle Airport

See separate guide.

Le Bourget Airport

See Charles de Gaulle guide.

Airlines

Aerocondor	Delta Air Lines
Aigle Azur	easyJet
airberlin	easyJet Switzerland
Airlinair	Egyptair
Air Algérie	Hex'Air
Air Burkina	Iberia
Air Caraïbes	Iran Air
Air Comores International	Jet4you
Air Europa	Karthago Airlines
Air France	L'Avion
Air Ivoire	MyAir
Air Malta	Norwegian Air Shuttle
Air Mauritanie	Royal Air Maroc
Air Méditerranée	SkyEurope
Air Nostrum	Syrian Arab Airlines
Air Sénégal International	TAP Portugal
Atlas Blue	Transavia
CCM Airlines	TUIfly.com
CityJet	Tunisair
Clickair	Turkish Airlines
Compagnie Aérienne du Mali	Twin Jet
CorsairFly	Volare Airlines
Cubana	

Hotels

Ibis Paris Orly Aéroport

Orly Aerogare Cedex, BP141 Paris 94541 ☒ +33 1 56 70 50 70 ☒ www.ibishotel.com

A standard, affordable Ibis hotel. Even-numbered rooms on the fourth floor in particular have great views of the northern runway. Aircraft can be read off even at night. A short walk to the terminal.

Hilton Paris Orly Airport

267 Orly Aerogare Cedex, Paris 94544 ☒ +33 1 45 12 45 12 ☒ www.hilton.com

The pricier option at Orly, but much more comfortable. Rooms at the back of the hotel give views of the Ouest terminal and taxiway leading to Runway 25. Rooms at the front have limited views of some stands. Free shuttle operates to the terminals.

Rome (Fiumicino/Leonardo da Vinci)
Italy

FCO | LIRF

Tel: +39 (0) 66 59 51
Web: www.adr.it
Passengers: 28.9 million (2006)

Overview

The main airport in the Italy's capital handles a large amount of international and domestic traffic. It is situated close to the coast where the original Roman port was located, and 35km from Rome itself.

Changes in Alitalia's operations at Milan Malpensa, particularly with regard to long-haul operations, has meant an increase in the airline's presence at Rome. This will only benefit the enthusiast here. Much of the long-haul fleet will pass through over a 48 hour period, and many of the European and domestic fleets will pass through regularly. The domestic MD-80 fleet are in abundance here on shuttle flights to other Italian airports. Additionally, Air One makes up a large amount of the traffic.

Most of the major European carriers pass through Rome incluinge a number of low-cost airlines. Long-haul flights are provided from Asia, Africa and North America by the usual large carriers on a daily basis.

For the enthusiast, a good road system hugs the perimeter of most of the airport giving views of most movements. Additionally, some locations in and around the terminal buildings offer glimpses of aircraft on the ground and opportunities for photography. As always, be aware that security personnel rarely look favourably on this pastime.

MAP

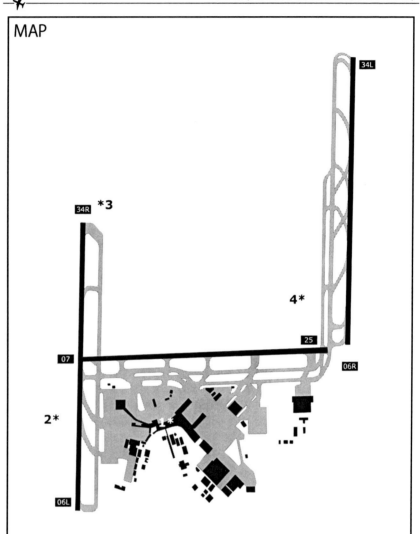

Frequencies

118.700 Tower
119.300 Tower
119.200 Approach
121.800 Clearance
121.900 Ground
114.900 ATIS
121.700 ATIS Departures

Runways

07/25   10,856x148ft / 3,309x45m
16R/34L 12,795x197ft / 3,900x60m
16L/34R 12,795x197ft / 3,900x60m

Spotting Locations

1. Terminal Cafe

Upstairs in Terminal B is a café known as the Terrazza Roma Gallerie. Large windows here overlook the aprons and two of the three runways. Most movements can be seen from here. Purchasing food and showing restraint when security personnel are around is a must.

2. Runway 06R/24L Road

Running the length of this runway is a road with many points along both sides where it's possibly to pull in and view aircraft. Photography is not really possible unless an aircraft has just lifted off. Be careful of traffic, and beware of police patrols. To reach this road, leave the terminal area in the direction of Fiumicino. You will soon pass the end of 24L and turn parallel to its length.

3. Runway 06R

Following the perimeter road from location 2, at the 06R end of the runway the road will bear right around a waterway. Around here are a number of places to pull in and watch aircraft passing overhead on short finals to the runway. Excellent for photography.

4. Between Runways

Following the perimeter road from the previous two locations, when you reach a T-junction, turn right. A number of spots here give views of aircraft on Runway 06L/24R. Continuing along the path will give you views of aircraft using Runway 25, and also across to the maintenance ramps. Beware this road leads to private properties, and is patrolled.

Airside Spotting

Spotting is possible airside in all three terminals, with windows around most gates, though parts of other terminals are not visible from the other. Keep an eye out for aircraft on runways and taxiways to catch what you've missed. The usual security presence exists throughout.

Resident Airframes

I-BUSM A300B2K ex-Alitalia
I-BUSN A300B2K ex-Alitalia
I-BUSQ A300B4 ex-Alitalia
I-BUSR A300B4 ex-Alitalia

Nearby Attractions

Ciampino Airport

Rome's other airport, situated closer to the city. It is a busy military and business aviation airport, with a number of low-cost operators flying throughout the day, including Ryanair and easyJet. There are a number of stored aircraft, and government transports.

Airlines

Adria Airways	Belle Air	Finnair	Qatar Airways
Aegean Airlines	Blu-express	FlyGlobespan	Royal Air Maroc
Aer Lingus	Blue1	FlyLal	Royal Jordanian
Aeroflot	Blue Air	Germanwings	Rossiya
AerolineasArgentinas	Blue Panorama	Iberia	SAS
Afriqiyah Airways	BimanBangladeshAirlines	Iran Air	Saudi Arabian Airlines
airBaltic	bmibaby	Japan Airlines	Singapore Airlines
airberlin	British Airways	Jat Airways	SkyEurope
Air Algérie	Brussels Airlines	Jet2	Sterling
Air Alps	Bulgaria Air	KD-Avia	SwissInternationalAirLines
Air Bee	Carpatair	KLM	Syrian Arab Airlines
Air Canada	Cathay Pacific	Korean Air	TACV Cabo Verde Airlines
Air China	China Airlines	Kuwait Airways	TAP Portugal
Air Europa	Clickair	LivingstonEnergyFlights	TAROM
Air Europe	Club Air	Libyan Airlines	ThaiAirwaysInternational
Air France	Condor	LOT Polish Airlines	TUIfly.com
Air Italy	Continental Airlines	Lufthansa	Tunisair
Air Malta	Croatia Airlines	Luxair	Turkish Airlines
Air Mauritius	CSA Czech Airlines	Malaysia Airlines	UkraineInternationalAirlines
Air Moldova	Delta Air Lines	MalévHungarianAirlines	United Airlines
Air One	DHL Airways	MATMacedonianAirlines	US Airways
Air Transat	Egyptair	MEAMiddleEastAirlines	Uzbekistan Airways
Air Vallée	El Al	Meridiana	Vueling
Albanian Airlines	Emirates	Montenegro Airlines	Wind Jet
Alitalia	Eritrean Airlines	MyAir	Wizz Air
American Airlines	Estonian Air	Niki	Yemenia
Austrian Airlines	Ethiopian Airlines	Norwegian Air Shuttle	Zoom Airlines
Belavia	Eurofly	Olympic Airlines	

Hotels

Hilton Hotel Rome Airport

Via Arturo Ferrarin 2, Fiumicino, Rome 00054 ☒ +39 (0) 66 52 58 ☒ www.hilton.com

This expensive hotel is connected to the terminal building and perfect for access. Certain rooms offer limited views of the domestic terminal ramp and taxiway. Aim for high floor rooms ending in 10.

Stockholm (Arlanda)
Sweden

ARN | ESSA

Tel: +46 (0) 87 97 60 00
Web: www.arlanda.se
Passengers: 17.9 million (2007)

Overview

Stockholm's main airport of Arlanda opened in 1960 some 26 miles north of the city. By 1983 it had completely replaced Bromma airport as the city's main gateway. The airport is one of the hubs of Scandinavian Airline System (SAS).

Arlanda has four terminals. Terminals 2 and 4 are used for domestic flights, whilst 3 and 5 are used for international flights. Arlanda Central was built to link with Terminal 5 and is used by SAS and its Star Alliance partners. There are also a number of cargo facilities and hangars at the airport.

There are three runways at Atlanda – the most recent opening in 2003. Enthusiasts are catered for near the recently-built runway 01L/19R with a covered building known as the Shed. Elsewhere views are possible around the airport.

The vast majority of movements at Arlanda are operated by SAS, including some by the long-haul fleet. Most European carriers frequent the airport, and a number of long haul airlines provide links with North America, Asia and the Middle East. Cargo carriers are also prominent, and if you are lucky you may visit when the airports preserved Caravelle makes its long-planned return to flight.

MAP

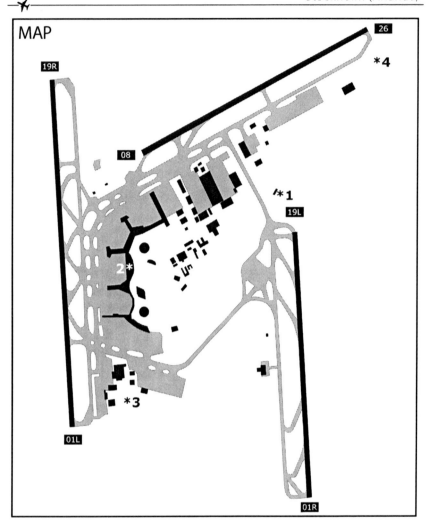

Frequencies

118.500 Tower RW01/19 & VFR Traffic
125.125 Tower RW08/26
128.725 Tower
119.400 Approach
120.500 Approach
123.300 Approach
121.700 Ground West
121.950 Ground North
121.975 Ground East
121.825 Clearance
119.000 ATIS Departures
121.625 ATIS

Runways

01R/19L 8,201x148ft / 2,500x45m
01L/19R 10,830x148ft / 3,301x45m
08/26   8,202x148ft / 2,500x45m

Spotting Locations

1. Spotters Shed

The only official location provided for the viewing of aircraft is a hut at the northern end of Runway 01R/19L. It also covers the de-icing area and taxiways linking with the runway. Aircraft can be seen at close quarters, and a good deal of movements read off. You can drive to the spot, or take bus line 593 from Terminal 5.

2. Sky City

The Sky City is located between terminals 4 and 5. It has large windows around the food court area which look out on to the aprons and Runway 01L/19R. The glass and sun position make photography difficult, but logging aircraft is not a problem.

3. Cargo Area

The cargo aprons, located to the south of the terminal complex, have a number of opportunities for close-up shots of aircraft parked. A car is useful, however a bus runs to this spot from the terminals. To drive her, take the main road away from the terminals towards Stockholm, but then take the first main exit and head towards the Cargo Terminal. At the next roundabout, turn right. Also around this area are opportunities to spot aircraft on short finals to Runway 01L.

4. Runway 26

Driving away from the airport, instead of taking the motorway to Stockholm, turn left on to the elevated road and head past the Spotters Shed and the Ibis Hotel on the 273. Just before the Ibis, turn left and follow the road until you can see the runway threshold and taxiway. This is a perfect spot for photographs if aircraft are using this runway.

Airside Spotting

Once airside, the terminals at Stockholm can be fairly rewarding. Most areas have large windows looking out over the gates and distant action on Runway 01L/19R. The glass and sun can make photography difficult.

Resident Airframes

SE-DAA Caravelle, ex SAS. Parked eastern apron. Tug trainer.
SE-DAF Caravelle, ex SAS. Parked eastern apron.
SE-DAI Caravelle, ex SAS. Engines maintained and regularly tested.
SE-DEC Caravelle, ex SAS. Poor condition on fire dump.
SE-CNK Viscount. Fire dump.

Nearby Attractions

Bromma Airport

This was the original airport for Stockholm, but limitations in its facilities saw most scheduled traffic move to Arlanda by 1983. Today it is used extensively by business jets, and has a number of regional air services by the likes of Malmö Aviation, Sun Air and Skyways. There is a viewing area at the terminal and a mound alongside. Roads around the perimeter are also good for watching movements.

Airlines

Adria Airways	Ethiopian Airlines	Nouvelair Tunisia
Aeroflot	Finnair	Novair
Aerosvit Airlines	FlyNordic	Pegasus Airlines
Air Adriatic	Fly Air	Qatar Airways
Air Åland	Free Bird Airlines	Rossiya
airBaltic	Germanwings	SAS
airberlin	Golden Air	Skyways Express
Air Caraïbes	Helvetic Airways	Spanair
Air China	Iberia	Sterling Airways
Air Europa	Icelandair	SunExpress
Air Finland	Iran Air	Swiss International Air Lines
Air France	Jat Airways	Syrian Arab Airlines
Arkia	Jordan Aviation	TAP Portugal
Atlantic Airways	KLM	Thai Airways International
Austrian Airlines	LOT Polish Airlines	TNT Airways
Blue1	Lufthansa	Transwede Airways
British Airways	Malaysia Airlines	TUIfly.com
Cimber Air	Malév Hungarian Airlines	TUIfly Nordic
Continental Airlines	Malmö Aviation	Turkish Airlines
CSA Czech Airlines	Nextjet	US Airways
Delta Air Lines	Niki	Viking Airlines
DHL Airways	Nordic Leisure	West Air Sweden
Eastern Airways	Nordic Regional	
Estonian Air	Norwegian Air Shuttle	

Hotels

Radisson SAS SkyCity Hotel

Stockholm Arlanda Airport, SE-19045 ☒ +46(0)850674000 ☒ www.radissonsas.com
Located above terminals 4 and 5. Rooms higher up and at each end of the building offer great views over the movements – particularly of Runway 01L/19R. Photography is not really possible, however. The hotel can be expensive.

Hotel Ibis Stockholm Arlanda

Lindskrog, vag 273, S-190 45 Arlanda ☒ +46 (0) 86 55 01 00 ☒ www.ibishotel.com
Offers shuttle to the terminal, which takes 10 minutes. The hotel is fairly affordable. Some rooms have distant views of aircraft on the runways, and some of the remoter stands. SBS users will have more luck identifying aircraft.

Toulouse (Blagnac)
France

TLS | LFBO
Tel: 0825 38 00 00 (within France)
Web: www.toulouse.aeroport.fr
Passengers: 6 million (2007)

Overview

Although itself only a regional airport with no traffic of particular note to the enthusiast, the big draw of Toulouse is the Airbus factory which churns out endless A320's, A330's, A340's and A380's destined for the far corners of the globe. Many of these are unlikely to be seen again in European skies for many years, if ever, and so proves incredibly tempting for the spotter.

Regular traffic at Toulouse involves a variety of domestic and European flights from Air France and other carriers, mainly by regional and medium-haul types. Movements are generally focussed around the rush hour periods.

Airbus traffic can be relied upon most days, with test flights operating regularly of the latest aircraft off the production line. Additionally, the recent airframes to emerge from the giant hangars can usually be seen in plentiful supply around the various aprons and maintenance areas around the airfield.

Many visitors choose to take a tour of the Airbus factory, which must be booked in advance. This gives the opportunity to see aircraft on the production line, including the massive A380.

In addition to Airbus, ATR also produce their turboprop airliners at Toulouse Airport. These can also often be seen on test and delivery flights, and receiving attention on the aprons.

A small aviation museum on the western perimeter has a number of preserved airliners on display.

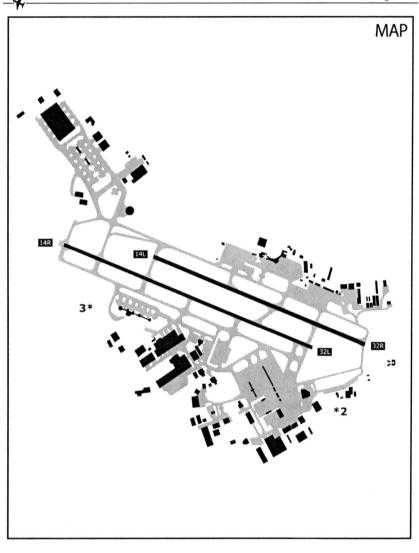

MAP

Frequencies

118.100 Tower
121.100 Surveillance Radar
121.250 FlightInformationService
121.700 Departures
121.900 Ground
123.125 ATIS

Runways

14R/32L 11,483x148ft / 3,500x45m
14L/32R 9,843x148ft / 3,000x45m

Spotting Locations

1. Airport Café and Viewing Deck

Inside the terminal building is a café on the second floor. Outside is a viewing deck provided for watching aircraft, with no charge. This gives views over the runways, taxiways, gates and the distant Airbus ramps. Photography is very easy here.

2. Car Park

On the southern perimeter amongst the Airbus side of the airport is a car park from which arrivals on runways 32L/R can be logged and photographed easily, and many of the Airbus ramps can be logged. This car park is reached along the perimeter road, and by passing the Airbus car parks along Chemin de la Crabe. A short walk will yield better results.

3. Hill

A large hill exists on the western (Airbus) side of the airport which overlooks all movements on the runways, particularly in the 14L/R direction. Photography and logging are possible here. To reach the spot, head north from the terminal building. At the Pizza Hut roundabout, cross the bridge and then follow the main road alongside the runway. Turn left at the next two roundabouts, and you'll eventually reach a dirt parking area and the hill.

Resident Airframes

F-BPPA Aero Spacelines Guppy preserved
F-WUAB A300B4 preserved
F-BVFC Concorde Air France preserved
F-WTSB Concorde preserved
F-GBOL DC-3 preserved
F-BTOE Caravelle Air Inter preserved
F-GHMU Caravelle Air Toulouse International preserved
+ many more at museum.

Nearby Attractions

Airbus Factory Tours

Village Aéroconstellation, Rue Frantz Joseph Strauss, 31700 Blagnac
– Follow signs for Parc Aéronautique Colomiers   ☒ +33 5 39 42 00   ☒ www.taxiway.fr

Tours of Europe's largest aircraft manufacturing site last around 1.5 hours and take in either the A330/A340 production line, or A380 production line. You must book in advance, bring a passport, and remember that photography is not allowed inside the buildings.

Toulouse Air Museum

183 rue Gaston Doumergue, 31170 Tournefeuille   ☒ +33 5 61 70 01   ☒ www.aatlse.org

Amongst the Airbus buildings on the western side of Toulouse Airport is a collection of historic aircraft. Amongst the airliners on display are a DC-3 and Caravelles. Another Caravelle and a Concorde production aircraft can be seen as part of the Airbus tour.

Airlines

Aer Lingus	Germanwings
Aigle Azur	Iberia
Air Algérie	Jet2
Air France	Karthago Airlines
Air Malta	LTE International Airways
Air Méditerranée	Lufthansa
Air Nostrum	Nouvelair
Air Transat	OLT
Atlas Blue	Onur Air
bmi	Royal Air Maroc
bmibaby	Spanair
British Airways	TAP Portugal
Brussels Airlines	Thomas Cook Airlines
CorsairFly	Tunisair
easyJet	Twin Jet
Europe Airpost	Viking Airlines
Flybe.	

Hotels

Campanile Hotel Toulouse Purpan

33 Route de Bayonne, Toulouse 31300 ☒ +33 5 61 16 90 90 ☒ www.campanile.fr

Although a few miles from Toulouse Airport's terminal, this affordable hotel does offer some views of aircraft on the runways, and the Airbus factory. Rooms ending in 11, 13, 17, 19, or 21 reputedly offer the best views.

Pullman Toulouse Airport

2 Avenue Didier Duarat, 31800 Blagnac ☒ +33 5 34 56 11 11 ☒ www.sofitel.com

Formerly the Sofitel. Rooms can be expensive, but the hotel is smart. Certain higher rooms have limited views of the terminal and remote aprons.

Vienna (Schwechat)
Austria

VIE | LOWW

Tel: +43 17 00 70
Web: www.viennaairport.com
Passengers: 18.8 million (2007)

Overview

Vienna Airport has in recent years enjoyed many positive reviews from enthusiasts who have made the journey, thanks to low-cost access, and a wealth of exotic movements.

Vienna's airport at Schwechat was constructed around a year before the start of World War 2 just as Germany took control of Austria and Lufthansa became the national carrier. During the war the Heinkel company took control of the airport to conduct flight testing of its new aircraft. The first hard runway was laid for this purpose, and the Allied forces inflicted serious damage to it on numerous occasions.

Following the war the airport was rebuilt for civilian use by the Allied occupation force. However, it was not until 1953 that the airport saw any significant growth. Now under the control of local authorities, the runway was extended and a new terminal built. In 1977 a second runway was opened to cope with increased traffic, and a new freight centre was opened in 1986 to cope with extra demand from cargo flights.

Today Vienna's airport handles primarily scheduled traffic to the main business and tourist cities around Europe, North America and Asia. Austrian Airlines provide the majority of flights, with much of their fleet passing through the airport on any given day.

For spotters, a few locations exist. Frustrating runway switches take place regularly, so be ready to move!

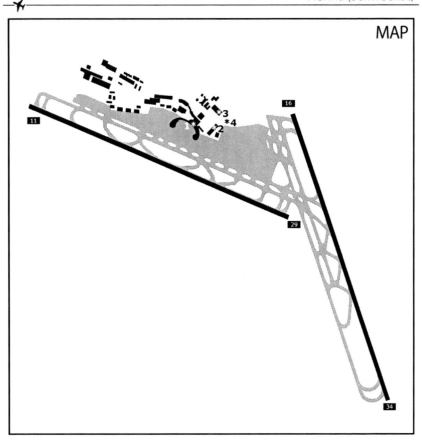

MAP

Frequencies

119.400 Tower
121.200 Tower
118.525 Approach VFR
119.800 Approach
124.550 Approach
128.200 Approach
129.050 Approach
122.125 Clearance
121.600 Ground
112.200 ATIS
113.000 ATIS
115.500 ATIS
121.725 ATIS Departures
122.950 ATIS

Runways

11/29	11,483x148ft / 3,500x45m
16/34	11,811x148ft / 3,600x45m

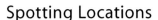

Spotting Locations

1. Terminal

The Balloon Café/Restaurant in the terminal is the primary place to get views of movements. Most traffic will pass this spot either on the way in or out, however it is quite restrictive.

2. Car Park 3

The top of the multi-storey car park number 3 is a popular spot for a general overview of the commuter aprons and some of the gates which widebodies park at. Clutter can spoil photographs at this spot. Some of the aircraft parked at the cargo and maintenance ramps can be logged from here.

3. Car Park 4

The top level of the multi-storey car park number 4 is situated alongside Runway 16/34. This is particularly good for logging and photographing aircraft using the 16 direction. You will also see a remote parking area alongside this car park which is hard to see from anywhere else. The new terminal extension partly obscures the view from this car park now.

4. Airport Tour

An airside tour is available from the VisitAir Centre adjacent to Car Park 4, which takes in the maintenance, general aviation, executive and passenger aprons. A security check is required. Tickets cost €7. The tour departs on the hour from 9am to 5pm, and lasts an hour. No tours on Sundays. Reservations on +43 17 00 72 21 50

Airside Spotting

Once airside in both terminals, there are windows around the departure areas which offer limited views of the stands and some runway movements.

Airlines

Adria Airways	Cyprus Airways	Luxair
Aeroflot	Delta Air Lines	Martinair Cargo
Aer Lingus	DHL Air	MAT Macedonian Airlines
African Safari Airways	Dniproavia	Mesopotamia Air
airBaltic	easyJet	Niki
airberlin	Emirates	Olympic Airlines
Air China	Emirates Cargo	Onur
Air France	Egyptair	Pegasus Airlines
Air Malta	El Al	Qatar Airways
Air Moldova	Estonian Air	Rossiya
Air One	EVA Air	Royal Jordanian
Air Transat	Finnair	SAS
Air Via	Free Bird Airlines	Saudi Arabian Airlines
Alitalia	Georgian Airways	SkyEurope
Asiana Airlines Cargo	Germanwings	Spanair
Austrian Airlines	Iberia	SunExpress
Belavia	InterSky	Syrian Arab Airlines
British Airways	Iran Air	Swiss International Air Lines
Brussels Airlines	Jat Airways	TAROM
Bulgaria Air	Jet Air	TNT Airways
Bulgarian Air Charter	KD-Avia	Transaero Airlines
Central Connect Airlines	KLM	Tunisair
China Airlines	Korean Air	Turkish Airlines
China Airlines Cargo	Korean Air Cargo	Ukraine International
Clickair	LOT Polish Airlines	Viaggio Air
Croatia Airlines	Lufthansa	

Hotels

NH Vienna Airport Hotel

Einfahrtsstrasse 1-3, Wien Flughafen 1300 ☒ +43 1 70 15 10 ☒ www.nh-hotels.com

The best hotel at Vienna Airport for views of movements. Odd-numbered rooms on the third floor will give views over the apron at the time of writing. Some other higher rooms have views over the 11/29 runway. The hotel is one of the more affordable at the airport. A short walk from the terminal.

Zurich (Kloten)
Switzerland

ZRH | LSZH
Tel: 41 (0) 43 816 2211
Web: www.zurich-airport.com
Passengers: 20.7 million (2007)

Overview

Zurich is a popular choice in Europe for aviation enthusiasts as it provides some excellent facilities, and has been the home of a well-stocked shop for many years.

The airport is somewhat of an anomaly in that it is the busiest airport in Switzerland, and yet it serves neither the capital city nor a large local population. It is the main operating base for national carrier Swiss, formerly Swissair, which has passed through turbulent times over the past decade, seeing fleet and passenger numbers dwindle. However, with German carrier Lufthansa's controlling stake, the airline has recently seen its fortunes turned around, and passenger figures at Zurich on the rise again.

Other airlines from across Europe, North America and Asia make up the numbers with daily flights, and an interesting mix of executive jets regularly occupy the ramps.

Every January, the World Economic Forum is held close to Zurich in the town of Davos. This brings in leaders from around the world, and their entourages of private jets, both big and small. Enthusiasts flock to Zurich every year for the feast of rare types and registrations.

The official viewing locations at Zurich are amongst the best in Europe. There are, however, some useful spots around the airport which can produce stunning photographs. Whilst movements are not as numerous as other European hubs, Zurich is worth a visit to clear the Swiss fleet in a short time.

MAP

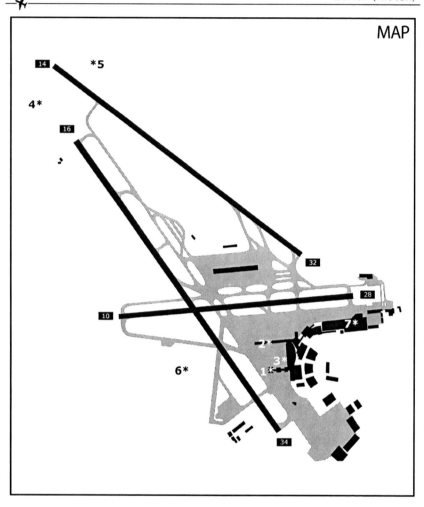

Frequencies

118.100 Tower
119.700 Tower/Arrivals
120.225 Tower RW24 ARR RW32 DEP
127.750 Tower
118.000 Arrivals
125.325 Finals
125.950 Departures
121.800 Clearance Delivery
121.850 Ramp
121.900 Ground
128.525 ATIS

Resident Airframes

TU-TCPDC-8-53, ex-Air Afrique fire trainer
EX-1146K IL-14, Runway 34 Restaurant

Runways

10/28	8,202x197ft / 2,500x60m
14/32	10,827x197ft / 3,300x60m
16/34	12,139x197ft / 3,700x60m

Spotting Locations

1. Pier B Terrace

The terrace on top of Pier B is the original and best spot for watching and logging aircraft movements at Zurich. Aircraft pass by and park very close to this location, making photography possible. The BUCHairSHOP is located here, along with a restaurant and refreshments. This terrace is signposted within the terminal.

2. Pier E Terrace

Another rooftop terrace, Pier E brings you a little closer to the runways and some of the gates not visible from Pier B. Photography is good. This position is reached via bus from the Pier B Terrace. There is an additional CHF4 charge for adults, CHF2 for children. This terrace is not open every day.

3. Guided Tours

A behind-the-scenes bus tour is available at Zurich. This leaves from the Pier B Terrace and takes in the Airside Centre, Piers A and B, Runway 28, nature reserve, cargo and maintenance areas, and the emergence services. Tour lasts over an hour and costs CHF8 for adults and CHF4 for children. Tickets can be bought from the terrace or e-mail visitorservices@flughafen-zuerich.ch

4. Runways 14 and 16

Two runways end close to each other at the far end of the airport to the terminal. Drive in the direction of Oberglatt. A short distance after this small town, find the large car park on your right. This spot can produce some stunning photographs with the Alps as a backdrop. Best in the afternoon, this spot is popular with locals.

5. Runway 14

Continue past the previous spot and turn right along a small road which leads to another car park. This spot allows better photography of aircraft on approach in the mornings.

6. Perimeter Fence

Opposite the terminal and Runway 16/34 is another famed spot at Zurich. It pits you amongst the action, with great views of traffic on the runways, and aircraft around the terminals. Photography is excellent from the afternoon, even with shorter lenses. To reach the spot, drive towards Oberglatt, but turn right just before the pedestrian bridge at Rümlang Station. Alternatively, bus route 510 from Car Park F leaves every hour. Get off at Rumlang Station. From Rümlang, walk through the tunnel, cross the footbridge and keep walking until you see the fence.

7. Car Park F

The top level of Car Park F gives good views over the commuter ramp and Runway 28 threshold and taxiways. Photography is good in the late morning and early afternoon from this spot.

Airside Spotting

All of the terminals and piers offer some views over the action. It can be frustrating as not all movements can be observed once you are in the departure lounges. You will certainly see aircraft parked around you, and aircraft taxiing to nearby runways.

Airlines

Adria Airways	bmi	Germanwings	Polar Air Cargo
Aer Lingus	British Airways	Hamburg International	Qatar Airways
Aeroflot	Bulgaria Air	Hello	Robin Hood Aviation
airBaltic	Cirrus Airlines		Rossiya
airberlin	CityJet	Helvetic Airways	Royal Air Maroc
Air Canada	City Airline	Iberia	Royal Jordanian
Air China	Clickair	Jat Airways	SAS
Air Malta	Continental Airlines	KLM	Singapore Airlines
Air Mauritius	Croatia Airlines	Korean Air	Spanair
Air France	Cyprus Airways	LOT Polish Airlines	SunExpress
Air One	CSA Czech Airlines	Lufthansa	SwissInternationalAirLines
Alitalia	Delta Air Lines	MATMacedonianAirlines	TAP Portugal
American Airlines	easyJet	Malév Hungarian Airlines	ThaiAirwaysInternational
Austrian Airlines	Edelweiss Air	Montenegro Airlines	TUIfly.com
Belair	El Al	Niki	Turkish Airlines
Belle Air	Emirates	Norwegian Air Shuttle	UkraineInternationalAirlines
B&H Airlines	Emirates Cargo	OLT	United Airlines
Blue1	Finnair	Onur Air	
Blue Islands	Free Bird Airlines	Pegasus Airlines	

Hotels

Park Inn Zurich Airport

Flughofstrasse 75, 8153 Rümlang ☒ +41 (0) 44 828 8686
www.zurich-airport.parkinn.com

If you request a room overlooking the airport, you won't be disappointed. Most of the action is visible from here, although photography is a little limited due to the distance and glass. This hotel can be fairly expensive.

NH Zurich Airport Hotel

Schaffhauserstrasse 101, 8152 Glattbrugg, Zurich
+41 (0) 44 808 5000 ☒ www.nh-hotels.com

Very affordable hotel a short distance from the terminals. Some rooms offer limited views of movements on Runway 16, but no photographic opportunities.

Nearby Attractions

Dübendorf Airfield Museum of Military Aviation

Überlandstrasse 255, 8600 Dübendorf ☒ +41 (0) 44 823 2017 ☒ www.ju-air.ch

A popular museum only a few miles from Zurich Airport. Has a number of military aircraft preserved in hangars. Also the opportunity to experience sightseeing flights on a restored Junkers Ju-52 aircraft.

LOW COST AIRPORTS

Frankfurt (Hahn)
Germany

HHN | EDFH

Tel: +49 (0) 65 43 / 5 09-1 13
Web: www.hahn-airport.de
Passengers: 4.1 million (2007)

Overview

Hahn Airport shot from relative obscurity as a former NATO base to one of Germany's busiest airports in a very short time following the investment of Fraport AG, who own Frankfurt Main Airport, and the decision by Ryanair to open a base here.

The latter was expanded rapidly, opening up this part of Germany (and neighbouring parts of France and Luxembourg) to low cost travel around Europe. Despite their insistence on naming this airport Frankfurt-Hahn, it is actually 75 miles from the city.

As well as low cost flights, which are also operated by Wizz Air and Iceland Express, the airport handles many cargo flights. Aeroflot-Cargo have a base here, and other airlines regularly bring Russian-built freighters in.

The modern terminal is not particularly good for spotting once airside, although the runway and adjacent stands are in sight.

There are a number of places where apron and runway views are possible around the perimeter road, and alongside the terminal complex.

Buses run hourly to Frankfurt train station and Frankfurt Main Airport.

Airlines

Aeroflot-Cargo
Air Armenia
Egyptair Cargo
Emirates Cargo
Gemini Air Cargo
Iceland Express
MNG Airlines
Polet Cargo
Ryanair
Vladivostok Avia
Wizz Air

Frequencies

119.650 Tower
120.900 Tower
125.600 Approach
121.975 Ground
136.350 ATIS

Milan Bergamo (Orio al Serio)
Italy

BGY | LIME
Web: www.orioaeroporto.it
Passengers: 5.2 million (2006)

Overview

Orio al Serio Airport is located on the southern edge of the city of Bergamo. It is considered Milan's third airport, and in particular the low-cost airline airport of the city.

Ryanair has a base here, and most of the other main low-cost airlines of Europe put in appearances in the schedules. Local airline MyAir has a large presence at the airport, and Italian charter airline Eurofly covers many of the holiday destinations. In addition to this, national carrier Alitalia maintains daily links to Rome Fiumicino.

Bergamo is also known as a cargo hub, and in particular a base for DHL and its nightly operations. Most aircraft types in their fleet visit, and it is not uncommon to see some subbed aircraft from other cargo carriers operating through the airport.

On the north side of the airfield is a general aviation base, and a storage area with a number of Fokker F-27 aircraft.

There are a number of opportunities to log and photograph aircraft here. The best spot is on top of the car park to the left of the modern terminal building. Additionally roads pass both ends of the main runway, and also lead to the General Aviation area. Airside spotting is also possible, although photography is not recommended.

Resident Airframes

F-WQVF Fokker F-27
HA-FAE Fokker F-27

Airlines

airberlin

Air Slovakia

Alitalia

Belle Air

Blue Air

Brussels Airlines

Carpatair

Club Air

DHL Air

Eurofly

Jet2

MyAir

Ryanair

SkyEurope

Transavia

TuiFly.com

UPS

Wizz Air

Frequencies

120.500 Tower
126.500 Tower
126.750 Departure
132.700 Approach
112.600 ATIS

Rome (Ciampino)
Italy

CIA | LIRA
Web: www.adr.it
Passengers: 6 million (2007)

Overview

Ciampino is Rome's original airport, and is located much closer to the city than the current primary airport at Fiumicino.

Although still used as an airbase and home for the country's military transport aircraft, Ciampino has developed itself into a busy low-cost gateway to the city. Since the arrival of Ryanair, and other airlines such as easyJet and Wizz Air, passenger figures have grown rapidly. DHL, UPS and TNT also provide cargo operations.

For the enthusiast, the airport is a gold mine with presidential transports, an abundance of executive jets, and many general aviation and Fire Fighter Canadair CL-215s in residence. However, due to the military presence and Italy's general suspicion towards aircraft enthusiasts, caution must be taken at all times.

From the car parks around the terminal, views can be had over the eastern ramp which usually covers the business jets, cargo aircraft and general aviation. A drive around the perimeter will open up some more opportunities. It is hardest to see the airliners and the runway from anywhere other than the departure lounge.

Resident Airframes

MM61898 Convair 440
MM61899 Convair 440
MM61901 Convair 440
I-DRIB Dassault Falcon 20
I-LIAC Dassault Falcon 20
MM62012 Douglas DC-9
UR-87592 Yak 40

Airlines

Centralwings

DHL Air

easyJet

Norwegian Air Shuttle

Ryanair

Sterling

TNT Airways

UPS

Wizz Air

Frequencies

120.500 Tower
122.100 Tower
130.900 Departures
119.200 Approach
119.400 Clearance Delivery
121.750 Ground
131.625 Apron

Shannon

Republic of Ireland

SNN | EINN
Web: www.shannonairport.com
Passengers: 3.6 million (2007)

Overview

Shannon has a long history of aviation and is one of the Republic of Ireland's three busiest airports. It has the longest runway in Ireland.

Traditionally Shannon served as a gateway to the Americas. Most airliners were forced to make a stop here since it was the last stop for fuel before crossing the Atlantic, and latterly because of a bilateral agreement whereby airlines must make a stop in Shannon even if serving Dublin. After years of disagreements, the Shannon Stopover, as it became known, was finally abolished in March 2008.

Over the years many airlines have served Shannon with aircraft that would not usually be seen in these parts. The days of these operations are now gone, although the visitor will still usually see a number of North American and European airlines each day. The airport is also regularly used for crew training, maintenance and aircraft storage.

Ryanair and Aer Lingus are the principal operators at the airport. Many enthusiasts take the opportunity to fly on an Airbus A330 between Dublin and Shannon for knock-down prices (the aircraft continues to New York).

There is an indoor gallery in the terminal building on the third floor, with views over all the movements but thick, dirty glass in place. There are also spots at the end of each runway where photography is possible.

Resident Airframes

N907RF Boeing 727, fire trainer

Airlines

Aer Lingus
Air Contractors
Air Europa
Air France Cargo
Air Transat
Centralwings
CityJet
Continental Airlines
Delta Air Lines
DHL Airways
Dubrovnik Airline
Futura Gael
Iberworld
Monarch Airlines
Onur Air
Ryanair
TNT Airways
UPS
US Airways

Frequencies

118.700 Tower
120.200 Approach
121.400 Radar
121.800 Ground
130.950 ATIS

Warsaw (Frederic Chopin)

Poland

WAW | EPWA

Web: www.lotnisko-chopina.pl

Passengers: 9.2 million (2007)

Overview

Poland has seen a massive boom in the number of flights to its airports with the advent of low-cost carriers such as Ryanair and Wizz Air. By far the largest and busiest airport in the country is Warsaw.

In addition to the low-cost airlines, national carrier LOT still plies its trade to many European destinations, and other European carriers make daily visits to the airport.

Warsaw provides an observation deck which is by far the best place for logging, and is good for photography until the afternoon. It is accessed from alongside the domestic terminal. There is a PLN4 entry fee for adults, and PLN2 for concessions. It is open from 6.30am to 8.30pm.

The best hotel at Warsaw is the Courtyard by Marriott. Asking for a room facing the airport will usually give good views over the aprons near the terminal. It can be quite expensive compared to nearby hotels, however.

Resident Airframes

SP-LHC Tupolev 134, police trainer
SP-LNB Ilyushin 14, fire trainer
SP-LNE Ilyushin 14, fire trainer

Airlines

Adria Airways	Finnair
Aer Lingus	FlyNordic
Aeroflot	Germanwings
Aerosvit Airlines	Iberia
Air China	Iceland Express
Air Europa	Jet Air
Air France	KLM
Air Italy	LOT Polish Airlines
Alitalia	Lufthansa
Austrian Airlines	Malév Hungarian Airlines
Belavia	Norwegian Air Shuttle
Blue1	Ryanair
bmibaby	SAS
British Airways	SkyEurope
Brussels Airlines	Sky Express
Centralwings	Swiss International Air Lines
Clickair	TNT Airways
CSA Czech Airlines	TUIfly.com
DHL Air	Turkish Airlines
Dniproavia	UPS
easyJet	Volare Airlines
El Al	White Eagle Aviation
FedEx Express	Wizz Air

Frequencies

118.300 Tower
128.800 Approach
121.600 Clearance Delivery
121.900 Ground
124.450 ATIS

Visit the...
AIRPORT SPOTTING BLOG
www.airportspotting.com

All of the latest news and guides to spotting at the world's airports, with regular updates on security measures, stored aircraft, trip reports, and hotels with views.

Contributions welcome from spotters.

Printed in the United Kingdom
by Lightning Source UK Ltd.
134797UK00001B/274-276/P